Hopi Silver

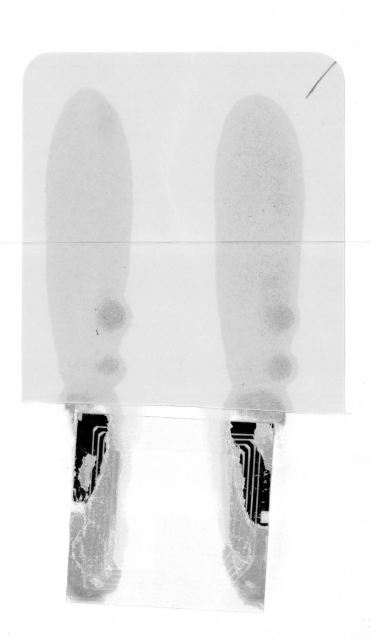

Cast jewelry by Preston Monongye in the "new Indian" style, 1970–71.

*The history
and hallmarks of
Hopi silversmithing*

HOPI SILVER

by MARGARET NICKELSON WRIGHT

Hopi hallmark drawings by Barton Wright

NORTHLAND PRESS / FLAGSTAFF, ARIZONA

Cover: Bracelet by Valjean Joshevema, 1949. Katharine Bartlett.

The author gratefully acknowledges the cooperation
of the Museum of Northern Arizona
in making available its materials and facilities.

Peter Bloomer, *Photographer*

International Standard Book Number 0–87358–097–4
Library of Congress Catalog Card Number 72–76377

Composed and Printed in the United States of America

To Barton, Elena, and Allen

Contents

Illustrations

Foreword

WHEN ONE HAS WATCHED research work taking place over a period of years, one cannot but hope to see the results published on the subject of that research. It is my pleasure to see such research come to fruition in this book by Margaret Wright.

Margaret and I have been visiting the Hopi pueblos together for a dozen years collecting for the Museum of Northern Arizona's annual Hopi Craftsman Exhibit. Both of us are interested in crafts, and Margaret was especially interested in the Hopis' silver jewelry.

I don't know exactly when it was that she began to make notes on Hopi silver, but I know that it was sometime ago when she began to carry with her on each trip a sheet of copper, and I found her talking to the Hopi silversmiths and asking them to hammer their silvermarks onto the sheet. Little by little Margaret collected the hallmarks of the silversmiths as well as different stamps that a silversmith may have used over the years. Then she began to look at our collections, noting the marks on the silver that we have in the Museum. After that, she began asking to look at friends' collections, and in seven years Margaret had most of the known Hopi silvermakers, when they worked, their marks, and who taught them. Then began the hard work — the writing of this book and the arduous job of tracking down a few nebulous Hopi silversmiths.

Her perseverance has resulted in getting almost all, if not all, of the marks and the history of the known silver craftsmen, no small feat when you realize that some worked for just a year or two and never worked in silver again.

It was with real pleasure that I found that Margaret felt she had all the information she could gather. I am also glad to know that the copper sheet will still accompany us on a few more trips while she gets some known, but unstamped, marks to add to this unique record.

I know of no other book that has traced the history of Hopi silver-crafting in such minute detail. Now collectors can look at their Hopi jewelry and by checking the marks in this book, find out who made it and perhaps when it was made.

EDWARD B. DANSON
Director, Museum of Northern Arizona

Preface

HOPI SILVER JEWELRY has been crafted over a period of seventy-five years, beginning just before 1900 and continuing today. By the mid-1930s some of the silversmiths had begun to mark their jewelry with a personal stamp which they referred to as a silvermark, but is commonly called a hallmark by collectors. No record was made of the marks for some years until Katharine Bartlett, Curator of History and Librarian at the Museum of Northern Arizona, began recording those available in the late 1950s. Several years later she gave her list to Barton Wright, Curator of the Museum, who added to it.

In 1965 I was asked to continue the research. In addition to making a drawing of each mark discovered, whenever possible, an impression of the mark was stamped into a copper sheet to make a permanent record for the Museum of Northern Arizona archives. Much of the data was gathered through visits to Hopi smiths or their families. The balance was given by knowledgeable collectors and scholars of Hopi silverwork. Eventually a fairly complete record of Hopi hallmarks was compiled.

The original purpose of the project was to add to the Museum's arts and crafts records, since through the years innumerable collectors of Hopi silver have turned to the Museum for identification of their pieces. However, in the process of gathering specific data on the silvermarks, a great deal of historical information emerged which both illuminated and enlarged the scope of the original research. It was felt the material should be made available to a larger audience and so the present form of the book was chosen. The material has been written as it was told to me. Since recollections of historical times tend to vary with the storyteller, there are likely to be other versions of some of the incidents.

Many people have helped with the compilation of information and preparation of the book. The Museum of Northern Arizona under its director, Dr. Edward B. Danson, has provided invaluable data through its collections and archives, and from its staff members. Hopi friends, Indian art dealers, collectors, and many others have generously given information and advice.

Two people have especially aided me. Katharine Bartlett assisted with the original Hopi silver project of the Museum of Northern Arizona in 1938 and has been associated with Hopi crafts for many years. She has freely given me advice and information. My husband Barton Wright has generously shared his extensive knowledge of Hopi people and their craftwork, as well as doing all the drawings for the Hopi hallmarks.

Doris Monthan has very ably and perceptively organized the manuscript and edited the book, for which I am deeply grateful.

Author's note: Hopi proper names have been hyphenated and accented in the body of the text to give the reader some help in pronunciation. Each vowel is usually sounded.

Introduction

THE UNIQUELY BEAUTIFUL silver jewelry made by Indians of the southwestern United States has been widely known and admired for the past hundred years. Though the Hopi people of northern Arizona acquired silvermaking at a later date than other tribes, they have developed a distinctive and fine quality jewelry that is equal artistically to that of any other people in the world.

From the beginning of Hopi silverwork around 1900, to the present, there have been skilled craftsmen actively producing silver jewelry. To more fully understand the development of Hopi silverwork, the growth of silversmithing among their neighbors and teachers, the Zuñi and Navajo, needs to be reviewed, as well as a brief history of other influences prior to the twentieth century.

In prehistoric times the southwestern Indians did no metalwork (and had no domesticated animals). It took over 250 years of European contact before they had both the need for and the opportunity to learn to work with metal.

The Spaniards were the first Europeans to contact the indigenous inhabitants of the Southwest. After settling in Mexico, the explorers and colonists moved northward in the 1500s through what are now Chihuahua and Sonora, and established colonies up the Rio Grande into the north of the present state of New Mexico and the southern part of Arizona. From here they moved out to other settlements; some were military outposts, others were civil communities, and still other settlements were religious missions. At first many of the Indian groups contacted did not openly object to the newcomers. Later

1

most of the tribes showed marked animosity toward them, which greatly diminished Spanish influence upon Indian culture.

It was many years after the Spaniards' arrival that the Indians acquired flocks of sheep, and still later that they had horses. After they obtained horses they had a greater need for metalwork so that they could make bridle bits, but the opportunity to learn to work with metal was still lacking. Arthur Woodward, in his book *Navajo Silver: A Brief History of Navajo Silversmithing,* stresses the point that smithing could not be learned "passing by" on a raiding party. There had to be opportunity for the Indians to observe the many vital steps in the making of metal objects, and perhaps even the chance to do some of the operation for themselves. He points out that a man would also have to obtain the necessary tools and the metal to work with before he could begin smithing for himself. Even if a skilled metal worker became a captive of the Indians, he could not teach them his craft without tools and metal.

The first record of a Navajo blacksmith appears about 1850. This man, Atsidi Sani, or Herrero (Iron Worker) as the Mexicans called him, became a silversmith as well. In *The Navajo and Pueblo Silversmiths,* John Adair recounts the story a Navajo tells about Atsidi Sani, ". . . He was the first Navajo to learn how to make silver, and my grandmother told me that he had learned how to work with iron before that. He learned how to do this from a Mexican by the name of Nakai Tsosi (Thin Mexican) who lived down near Mt. Taylor. He [Atsidi Sani] thought he could earn money by making bridles. In those days the Navajo bought all their bridles from the Mexicans, and Atsidi Sani thought that if he learned how to make them the Navajo would buy them from him . . ." (Adair 1946, p. 4).

Referring to Atsidi, Woodward quotes from an 1865 government report, "Don't know whether the young men could repair the ploughs or not; [Herrero] is a blacksmith, and from him some of the young men have learned. Herrero Delgadito works in iron — makes bridle bits . . ." (Woodward 1971, p. 24).

It is the Mexican teacher at Mt. Taylor who is most often mentioned. However, Woodward also notes that in 1853 at Ft. Defiance,

2

Arizona, there was another Mexican silversmith working as an assistant to an American blacksmith, and that Atsidi Sani visited their forges. In an article for *El Palacio,* October 1928, Frederick Webb Hodge writes of a trader on the Navajo Reservation in the 1800s, who told of Mexican silversmiths coming around each year and making up silver for the Navajos in exchange for their horses. These men, who must have influenced Navajo silversmiths, are all called "Mexican" and it is likely, that to the Navajo, they were truly removed, in custom as well as time, from the hated Spanish conquerors of the past.

Metalwork was probably adopted by the Zuñi Pueblo Indians of western New Mexico around 1850, at approximately the same time the Navajo began to learn the craft. Adair places the making of brass and copper jewelry at Zuni in 1830 or 1840, though he does not give his source of information. There is a drawing of a Zuñi blacksmith shop (Cover illustration, *El Palacio,* October 1928) in Sitgreave's report of his 1852 visit, but there is no mention of metalwork in the text. A man called Ax Maker (Kiwashinakwe) who mended axes and hoes, is called the first Zuñi backsmith (Adair, p. 121).

James Stevenson, collecting Zuñi artifacts for the Smithsonian Institution in 1879, obtained a sandstone mold for "shaping metal into such forms as suit the fancy of the Indians for bridle and other ornaments; . . . Silver which has long been a metal of traffic among these tribes, is the one which is usually melted down for ornamental purposes. After it is taken from the mould it is beaten thin, then polished" (Stevenson 1883, p. 342, fig. 356). He also collected pottery crucibles "for reducing silver and copper in the manufacture of ornaments" (Stevenson 1884, p. 574).

A Zuñi man who spoke Navajo and was called Lan-ya-de has said that around 1872 a Navajo smith stayed with him and, in exchange for a horse, taught him to work silver. The Navajo taught him how to make dies so that he was able to make his own set of tools. In the next ten years other Zuñi men who had done brass and copper work learned to work silver from him (Adair, p. 122–123).

3

Once the basic techniques of metalworking were learned and the essential tools were made, traded for, or bought, a man could increase his own skill and improve his silverwork with continued practice. The craft could also spread among others in the tribe as long as there was a demand for the jewelry. This happened among both the Zuñi and Navajo, who gradually increased the output of silver jewelry for their native markets until the 1900s. Then the demands of the white tourists for Indian jewelry made many changes in the economics of silvermaking for the Zuñi, whose village lay near the railroad, and for those Navajo who lived near marketing outlets.

The silverwork of both tribes was similar in appearance in the late 1800s — it was heavyweight, and when set with turquoise, only a few large stones were used. For their silver, the smiths melted down American silver coins until about 1890, when government officials bcame strict about defacing United States money. At that time, most of the men began to use Mexican pesos which some of the traders kept in supply for the smiths.

Thus, at the time the Hopis acquired silversmithing, their neighbors were making massive jewelry, sometimes set with large turquoise stones, but still without individual tribal style. The Hopi smiths readily became skillful at working the metal but, as with the Navajo and Zuñi, it took thirty or forty years to develop a distinctive style of silverwork.

I

Hopi Crafts and Culture: 1500-1890

THE HOPI INDIANS of northeastern Arizona still live in towns they were inhabiting in the 1500s and practice a religion little changed by the white man. Their homes of stone are scattered about on the top, or just at the foot of sheer mesa cliffs surrounded by miles of sandy desert land. From this land they harvest abundant fruit and vegetables, and particularly corn, the grain that is the center of their lives. This harvest is possible only when they fulfill their duties in the relationship with their many supernatural beings or *kachinas.* They still work at many crafts — pottery, basketry, and weaving, which were necessities to them in their Stone Age life before A.D. 1500 but are now thought of as beautiful art forms.

Before contact with Europeans, the Hopis did no metalwork. For cooking they used pottery and stone; for cutting tools and for farming they used stone; for fastenings they used leather, sinew, and plant fibers. Jewelry was made from bone, wood, shell, colored stones (including turquoise), and seeds.

The Hopi towns have long been picturesquely located on three high mesas in Arizona that project like fingers from the southern end of the immense Black Mesa. In the late 1800s there were three villages to the east on First Mesa. They were Walpi, Sichomovi, which was an outgrowth of Walpi, and Hano, inhabited by Tewa people from the Rio Grande in New Mexico, who fled there after the Pueblo Rebellion of 1680. On Second Mesa there were Shungopavi, Mishongnovi, and Shipaulovi. On Third Mesa there was only the large village of Oraibi, known as the oldest continuously inhabited town in the United States because of its location at the same site from around A.D. 1150. Farthest to the west was the farming outpost of Moencopi. At the end of the 1800s people were just beginning to move to the foot of the mesas at Polacca and Kiakochomovi (New Oraibi).

While the Hopis were much more remote from European settlements than some other Indian groups, by the 1890s there were numerous changes to be seen in their lives. They had acquired many additions to their agriculture — new vegetables and fruits, especially the peach, flocks of sheep, as well as burros and horses. Missionary efforts by various groups had met with little success until this time, when Mennonite converts were made at Oraibi. There was a Baptist mission at Mishongnovi, and a Mormon colony at Moencopi; the latter was moved out by the government in 1907. Some schooling was being enforced by the government, at times through such drastic action as tying up the men and cutting off their hair unless they sent their children to school.

The issue of cooperating with the white men caused much trouble in the village of Oraibi, along with dissension about the presenting of their religious ceremonies. Bad feelings between the Conservative (those who held to Hopi tradition and beliefs) and Progressive (those who cooperated with the government) factions in the village finally resulted in the two groups attempting to perform important religious observances in duplicate. The quarrel was resolved on September 8, 1906, when the two factions came together outside the village. The Conservative leader, Yukioma, drew a line on the ground and said that whoever pushed him over it would be the winner. All the men (the boys were not allowed to join in for fear they would be injured) pushed against one another until finally Yukioma and his followers were forced far over the line and were declared the losers. They were permitted to take such of their belongings as they could carry and had to leave that day. Bloodshed was prevented by many of the relatives who, while politically siding with the Progressive faction, were grieved to lose their close relations — sons, daughters,

6

mothers, fathers, husbands, or wives. Age made no difference; even blind old people were led away and their houses ripped apart by the remaining villagers.

The people moved to a sandy area with a good spring, called Hotevilla, about eight miles across the mesa from Oraibi, and established a new village there. The next year some of the people wanted to move back to Oraibi but were refused, so they formed still another village at a place nearby, called Bakabi, which also had a spring.

At the end of the 1800s skilled Hopi artisans continued to produce a quantity of craft work. Metal cooking utensils had not yet replaced pottery, so it was still made by the women from all three mesas. But before too long a time, pottery making was to die out completely at the villages of Second Mesa, and on Third Mesa was to be represented only by undecorated culinary ware. Now the women of First Mesa are considered the only Hopi potters.

Many types of basketry were made by Hopi women. Utilitarian baskets of coarse wicker and of yucca were made in all the villages. The Oraibi women and the women who lived in the seceding Third Mesa villages were noted for flat wicker plaques made from rabbit brush dyed many colors. Women from Second Mesa specialized in coiled basketry made by wrapping bundles of galleta grass with thin strips of yucca leaf. The bundle was coiled into a spiral and sewn together with the yucca as it was bound. Different colors of yucca were used in the sewing to make stylized designs on the resulting flat plaques.

Hopi men were especially adept at fashioning intricate masks, as well as the complex religious paraphernalia for their kachina and other ceremonies. In addition they did all the weaving necessary to furnish the Hopi household with textiles. At the end of the nineteenth century the majority of Hopi women still wore native dresses. All the religious dances required native handwoven garments, and there was a large trade with all the Pueblos in New Mexico for the Hopi textiles.

These textiles provided the main trade goods used by the Hopi

7

to obtain the silver jewelry they wore before 1890. The Zuñi and Navajo jewelry was used exclusively until close to the 1900s, when a small amount of silver jewelry was crafted by Hopi men. While the men had made jewelry from shell, turquoise, and wood, they were not experienced with metalwork.

Plate 1. Sikyatala (Yellow Light), ca. 1902, by Jesse H. Bratley. Smithsonian Institution National Anthropological Archives neg. no. 53,447.

9

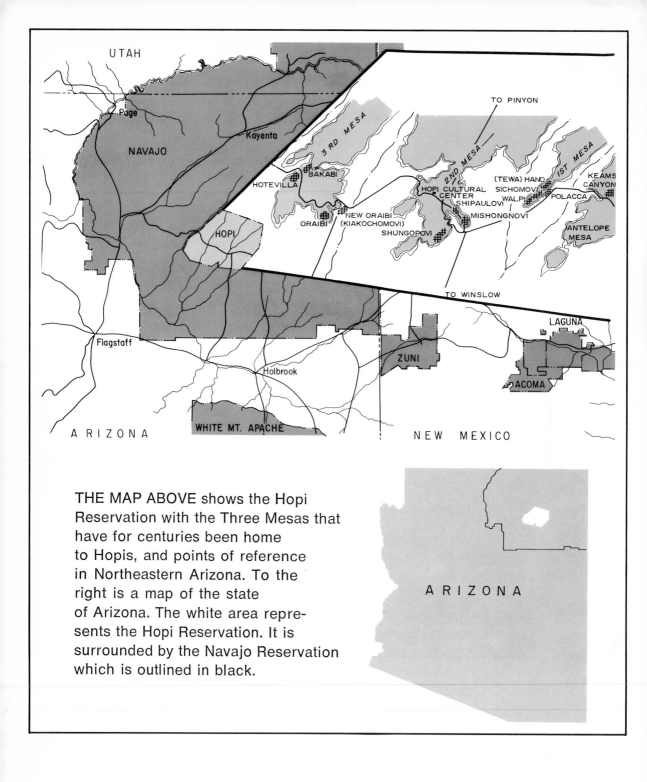

THE MAP ABOVE shows the Hopi Reservation with the Three Mesas that have for centuries been home to Hopis, and points of reference in Northeastern Arizona. To the right is a map of the state of Arizona. The white area represents the Hopi Reservation. It is surrounded by the Navajo Reservation which is outlined in black.

II

Early Hopi Silversmiths

1890–1910

IN 1906 when Hotevilla split from Oraibi, there were men from all three mesas doing silverwork. The jewelry these silversmiths have left shows their ability as craftsmen and a talent for design. The style reflects the general tradition of silverwork of the Indians of the Southwest during the last half of the nineteenth century, with elements drawn from Plains Indian metalwork, Spanish metal and leather work, as well as their own motifs and backgrounds.

These first Hopi smiths continued to make this style of jewelry for the next thirty years, as did new workers who learned the craft, but it was made only for Hopi use. When the smiths worked for commercial outlets the type of silver produced, as well as the style of design, was modified by economic demands. This did not intrinsically mean poor jewelry — in some cases the silverwork probably improved. But a smith called upon to make up a large quantity of less expensive bracelets in a short time obviously could not turn out work as well crafted and individually designed as a smith who made only a few bow guards and *concha* belts during a year. Too, the requests from tourists and traders for "Indian" designs, such as realistic bows and arrows and thunderbirds, did not foster the use of the more subtle Indian approach to these objects, or others drawn from their own mythology.

In a 1939 article for the *Plateau* bulletin, Mary-Russell Colton noted that after 1890 the Zuñi trader and silversmith, Lan-ya-de met with a Hopi trader, Sikyá-tala (which means Yellow Light: the yellow glow at sunset, the yellow of a sea of flowers in a field, the gold of a sunrise). The trading route was by foot over a trail 100 miles long. Whether they were at Hopi or Zuñi, by varying accounts, Sikyá-tala learned from the Zuñi man to make silver (Plate 1). Since there were regular trading relations between the two tribes, the sharing of silversmithing techniques would not have been strange, especially with a Hopi man of the Mustard Clan, which had Zuñi associations. Yellow Light obtained his own tools and made rings, bracelets, and hollow beads at the least (Colton: 2, 3; Adair 1944: 173, 176). He must have learned to solder along with the other smithing skills. The photograph of his workshop at Sichomovi, taken in 1911 by Samuel Barrett, shows a permanent forge with large bellows, crucibles and ladles of several kinds, a handmade set of balances, and possibly even a draw plate for making wire (in the upper right corner of the forge), as well as a small anvil and vise (Plate 1A). With such a permanent smithing shop, it is likely that he was able to make any of the jewelry in style at the time, including bow guards and *concha* belts. It is impossible to know whether he made cast jewelry, since the mold shown is used solely for casting an ingot to be hammered out, though his contemporary, Duwá-kuku, certainly was skilled at cast jewelry sometime in his life, as evidenced by his existing pieces.

Duwá-kuku, the father of a modern Hano potter, Garnet Pa-vá-tea, was also a silversmith at Sichomovi. In Alexander Stephen's *Hopi Journal,* he was mentioned as belonging to a Hopi society in 1891, so he was active in the ceremonial life of the village at the same time as Yellow Light, and was of the same Mustard Clan. He may well have been doing silverwork before 1900, and perhaps worked with Sikyá-tala. His cast bow guard, which is undated, shows skill both in the casting and in its inspired design (Plate 2).

Two Second Mesa men, Tawá-nimp-tewa and Tawá-hong-niwa, are said to have learned how to make jewelry from Yellow Light. Tawá-nimp-tewa, described by the Hopi as a small man, did silversmithing at Grand Canyon Village for some years. In the village of Shungopavi he is recalled not as a silversmith but as the first person to put a Shalako kachina design on a coiled plaque. It seems that some of the men in Shungopavi decided 'that they, as well as the

12

Plate 1A. Forge and smithing tools of Sikyatala, 1911 by Samuel Barrett. Milwaukee Public Museum.

Plate 2. Cast bow guard of Duwakuku and a sandstone mold. Date unknown. Hunter's Trading Post.

women, could weave coiled baskets. Several of them, including Tawá-nimp-tewa, proceeded to do just that, working at their homes rather than at the kiva. According to the Hopi, they were able to make "pretty good ones." One of Tawá-nimp-tewa's last pieces of silver, a bow guard, was made around 1930, though he lived until 1953.

Tawá-hong-niwa had five sons who soon learned jewelry making, and his only daughter's grandson, Valjean Lomá-heft-tewa, many years later after World War II, studied under the G.I. Bill and became a good silversmith. Tawá-hong-niwa and his sons were among the Second Mesa people who took part in the quarrel at Oraibi in the 1900s. After the Hotevilla people were forced to leave, United States soldiers arrested many of their men. Tawá-hong-niwa was imprisoned at Florence, Arizona. His five sons, as well as Andrew Humí-quap-tewa, all of whom were married, were sent to Carlisle Indian School

14

Plate 3. *Concha* belt made by Joshua before 1934.

15

in Pennsylvania. Tawá-hong-niwa was kept in prison about a year and a half, and the others returned from Carlisle some two years later, about 1910 (Nequatewa, *Truth of a Hopi,* 1936: 74, 76, 133).

The daughter of Tawá-hong-niwa's oldest son, Joshua, says that her father started his silverwork at Carlisle Indian School. He was proficient enough to demonstrate Hopi silversmithing for a week in San Diego in 1915. His work is illustrated by a *concha* belt (Plate 3). Joshua later married an Isleta woman and died in New Mexico.

There is little information about the next son, Lomá-wunu, who the Hopi say died "a long time ago." But we do have Barrett's 1911 photograph of him, dressed up for the occasion, with his silver tools and a pile of coins around him (Plate 4). He must have died a year or so after the picture was taken. Silas Kewań-wyma, the third son (called Silas Yma), made jewelry for the first Hopi Craftsman Show in Flagstaff in 1930, but died the next year.

The fourth son, Rutherford, toured the United States in 1935 and 1936 as a Hopi silversmith. A Mr. Billingsley from Phoenix had a troupe of Hopi dancers and demonstrators, including a Hopi silversmith and a basket maker, but no potter. They went to fairs, exhibits, and department stores, Sears Roebuck as well as others, traveling from Canada to Florida and visiting such cities as Detroit, Chicago, and Memphis. They camped out at all the places, and in Washington, D.C. slept on the Mall. Rutherford, a widower, had two children who traveled with him, his daughter demonstrating coiled basketry. In Syracuse his son was run over and killed by a car. When Rutherford returned from the trip in 1936, he stopped making silver and went to live with his brother Joshua in Isleta (Plate 5).

Washington Talaý-ump-tewa, the fifth son, was an active smith until his death in 1963, and entered jewelry in many of the Museum of Northern Arizona Hopi Craftsman Shows. The last year his entries were all turquoise-inlay wooden earrings, based on motifs going back to prehistoric times.

Andrew Humí-quap-tewa, another Shungopavi man who was sent to school at Carlisle, was a blacksmith who taught himself silverwork. His son, Paul Saufkie, whom he instructed, was later to be-

Plate 4. Lomawunu, Hopi silversmith of Second Mesa, 1911, by Samuel Barrett. Milwaukee Public Museum.

come the teacher for the World War II veterans' classes in silversmithing, which are described later. Paul tells that his father first worked with copper and brass, and that there is a big brass hoe made by him still in existence. Sometime after the railroad reached Williams, Arizona, Humí-quap-tewa would ride the train there, then walk on to meet the Havasupai to trade silver bracelets he had made for buckskins. Sometimes he would use colored bits of glass as sets in the bracelets, for turquoise was too scarce to use.

On Third Mesa, a man named Saké-wy-ump-tewa, and known as Sakwiam, told Adair that he learned silversmithing by watching Yellow Light from First Mesa, "I asked Sikyá-tala [Yellow Light] to make a necklace of hollow beads for me. I watched him make those beads and paid him fifteen dollars for them. I saw just how he used his tools and melted the silver. Then I tried it myself. It wasn't long before I could make simple pieces like buttons and rings. A few years later I moved from Oraibi to Hotevilla . . ." (Adair: 176). Today Hopi people remember Saké-wy-ump-tewa by his nickname *Sió*

17

Plate 5. Child's bow guard and bracelet by Rutherford.

which means *the Zuñi,* "because he spent a lot of time there." It is likely that he watched various silversmiths at Zuni and, perhaps, obtained their help in perfecting his craft.

Two half-brothers, Sak-hoí-oma and Dan Koch-ong-va, knew how to work with silver before they left Oraibi for Hotevilla at the time of the Split in 1906. Dan, who acted as one of the leaders of the Conservative men of Hotevilla, did silverwork until about 1940. He died in 1972. His brother, who entered silver jewelry in the Museum of Northern Arizona's Hopi Craftsman Show as late as 1950, was awarded a prize in 1948 for an entry at Flagstaff.

Before 1906 two cousins from Oraibi began to learn the silversmithing which they were to use throughout their lives. Ralph Tawang-yaouma and Pierce Kewan-wy-tewa (Plate 6) melted the solder off tin cans and used it to practice silverwork. They may have had some help with their silvermaking from Sío, who was from a related clan (Whiting 1942:16). Ralph moved to Hotevilla at the Split and then for many years was a full-time silversmith in Phoenix at Vaughn's and Fred Wilson's Trading Post, and in Tucson. Since his

18

Plate 6. Pierce Kewanwytewa demonstrating silverwork at the 1937 Museum of Northern Arizona Hopi Craftsman Show. Museum of Northern Arizona.

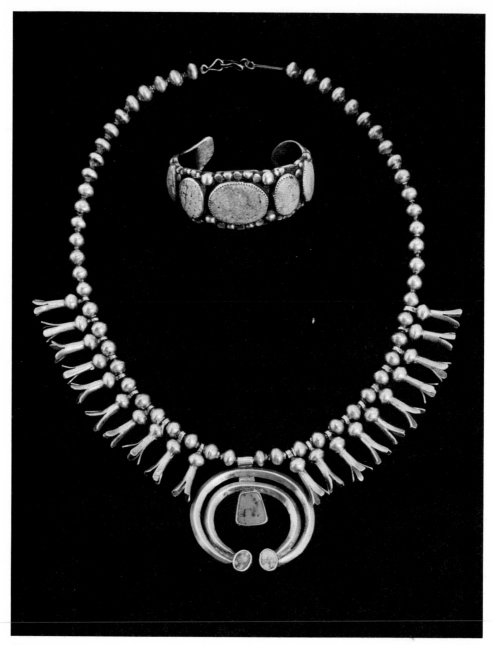

Plate 7. Bracelet, probably made in the 1920s, and squash blossom necklace, 1957, by Ralph Tawangyaouma.

20

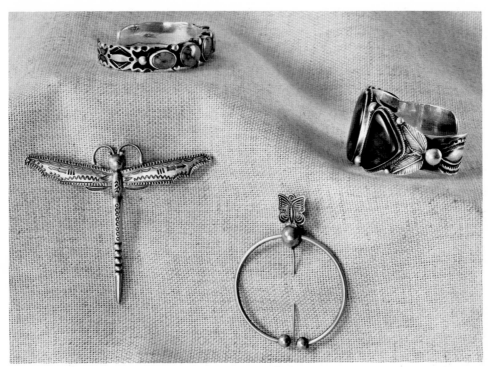

Plate 8. Upper bracelet by Ralph Tawangyaouma, 1943. Morris Robinson made the bracelet set with blue azurite in 1937, the dragonfly and butterfly pins ca. 1941.

retirement, he has moved back to Hotevilla where he is active in the ultra-Conservative group in the village, but still makes some jewelry. The pieces of his that I have seen were of heavy silver set with large stones. The turquoise was usually good and the pieces were well proportioned (Plates 7 & 8). Pierce's work was similar in appearance, though perhaps not as well finished. He did not work for a store, at least for any length of time, but continued the silversmithing part time, even after he married a Zia woman and moved to her New Mexico pueblo.

A *kik-mong-wi,* or village chief, of Oraibi was also a silversmith. Bert Fredericks acted as one of the chiefs of Oraibi from 1906 to 1910, while his brother, Tawá-quap-tewa, was forced to go to school

21

in California. It was Fredericks who refused the dissatisfied settlers from Hotevilla readmission to Oraibi, and forced them to go on to form the new village of Bakabi. He had been away at school himself and was called home to help during the Oraibi disagreement. Some say he learned silverwork at school. Fredericks worked at various trades including shoe repairing but continued the jewelry making as well, and had a small shop in Flagstaff for some years before his death in the 1960s. He specialized in squash blossom necklaces and *concha* belts.

SILVERSMITHS: 1910 - 1940

The village of Moencopi was a farming outpost of Oraibi near the present Tuba City. After the Oraibi-Hotevilla Split in 1906, many more people came to Moencopi. Several of these men became excellent silversmiths. Earl Num-kin-a started silvermaking in the 1920s and taught several younger men the craft. He quit smithing in the 1940s when his eyes went bad.

Frank Nu-taí-ma began silverwork sometime before 1920 and became very proficient in both cast and wrought silver (Plate 10). A *concha* belt of his in the Museum of Northern Arizona collections is made with smaller *conchas* but shows the same fine workmanship. Nu-taí-ma worked until the 1940s, and was blind for some fifteen years before his death in 1966.

Another smith from Moencopi had a short but productive professional life. From before 1924 Grant Jenkins worked at shops in Phoenix, including Graves Indian Store, Skiles, and Vaughn's. Later he was employed by Browns Jewelers in Flagstaff. Before his death in 1934 or 1935, he had assisted at least two Hopi men, Morris Robinson and Randall Hon-wiś-i-oma, to become full-time silversmiths.

Harold Jenkins, who was Grant Jenkins' first cousin, did silverwork for about fifteen years after first receiving some instruction from his wife's brother, Frank Nu-taí-ma.

Morris Robinson (Talá-wy-tewa) was born at Oraibi, but moved to Bakabi when that village was established. He lived with his cousin

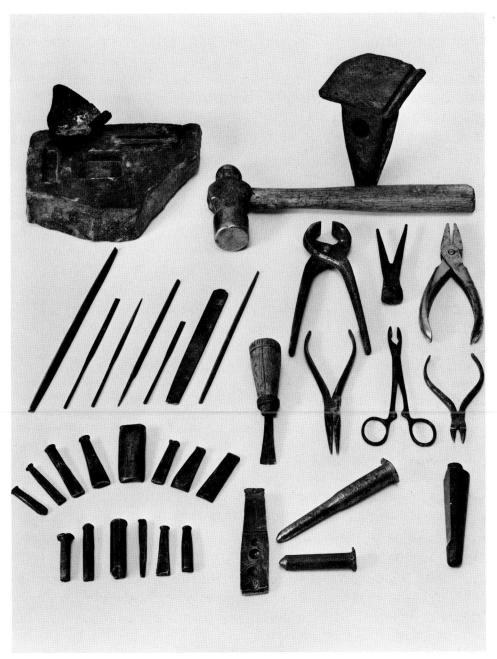

Plate 9. Duwakuku's silversmithing tools. Hunter's Trading Post.

23

Plate 9A. Duwakuku's dies or stamps. Hunter's Trading Post.

Grant Jenkins in Phoenix in 1924 and learned some of the rudiments of silverwork. In the 1930s he went to work for Skiles Indian Store in Phoenix. In later years he worked in other shops in Phoenix and Scottsdale. At first he made plain bracelets from a strip of silver set with turquoise and decorated with stamped designs at the ends. His skill increased until he was proficient in most silvercrafting techniques. He made any form of silver that would sell, from candlesticks and bowls to all types of jewelry. To make a bowl he took a large circle of 14-gauge silver and, using an old cannonball as a form, gradually hammered the silver into shape. At first he decorated the bowls with just a simple stamped border, but his work became increasingly more intricate as is shown in the illustrations. He used stamp de-

Plate 10. *Concha* belt, bow guards, and bracelets by Frank Nutaima between 1920 and 1940. Museum of Northern Arizona.

signs in many varied ways (Plate 8) and went on to use the chisel and stamp work as embellishments on overlay work (Plate 11). He also cast some silver, as illustrated by the belt buckle (Plate 11). Robinson retired in the 1960s and returned to Bakabi to help his brother tend their sheep. He brought a large stock of jewelry back with him, which he has been gradually selling. His tools are set up at his workbench and he makes jewelry now whenever he wishes.

Randall Hon-wiś-i-oma from Mishongnovi on Second Mesa worked as a silver craftsman in Williams, Arizona for a number of years. He first did silversmithing with Grant Jenkins at Graves Indian Store in Phoenix and moved to Williams in 1937. He was employed by

Vaughn's Indian Store until 1962, when deteriorating eyesight caused his retirement. A widower, he is now practically blind and lives by himself in a pretty white house in Williams.

A resident of Hotevilla since its establishment in 1906, Gene Nuvá-hoi-oma worked with silver for many years. His two sons, Rex and Allen, learned from him, and Allen has gone on to become a full-time silversmith, working for many years in Tucson for the McDaniels at the Santa Rita Indian Shop. Two years ago he moved to Holbrook, where he continues to make jewelry for sale.

Paul Saufkie of Shungopavi first worked silver in the 1920s under the tutelage of his father, Andrew Humí-quap-tewa. He was a capable blacksmith who became proficient in making both cast and hammered silver. After World War II he instructed veterans' silversmithing classes. He has run a store on the outskirts of Shungo-pavi for a number of years and that, together with the great amount of weaving he has done recently to provide his numerous sons with wedding robes for their wives, has kept him from making much jewelry for the past fifteen years. Now he has started smithing again and hopefully will continue (Plates 21, 27 & 36).

In 1930 several Hopi Indians were employed at San Gabriel, California as actors. They portrayed Mission Indians in a play presented at the mission. In their off hours, Earl Num-kiń-a worked on his silver jewelry. His nephew, Willie Coin of Oraibi, watched awhile and then asked to be taught how to do it. He became skilled at the work and has continued to practice the craft to the present, when he has time. However, he is also a weaver and is often busy at his loom. His work in the 1940s reflects the change in Hopi jewelry that was taking place then, even though he had no connection with the Museum of Northern Arizona silver project or the veterans' classes (Plate 12). Most of the jewelry Willie Coin fashions now is over-lay style. One of his more contemporary pieces is the *bolo* tie (Plate 36). He hopes to retire from his job at the Museum of North-ern Arizona before too many years and, perhaps, then will have more time to spend on silvermaking.

In the late 1930s, Frieda Santiago, a Hopi girl from Oraibi, watched

26

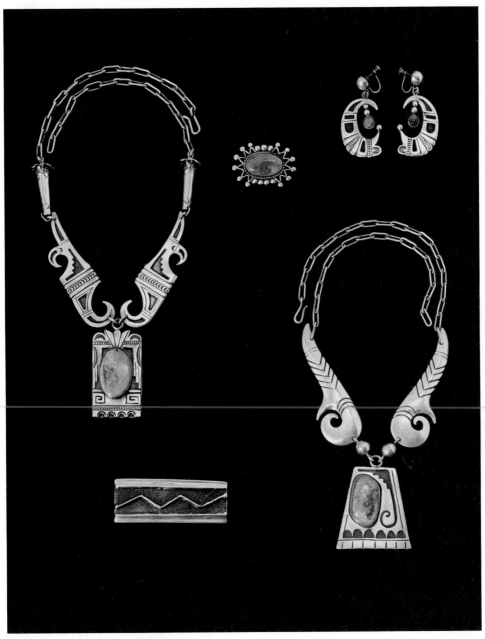

Plate 11. Silver set with turquoise by Morris Robinson, 1950–1960.
Buckle is cast. Museum of Northern Arizona.

her relative, Willie Coin, work on his silver. She learned how to do some things and then moved to Flagstaff, where she married a Zuñi man. The two of them made Zuñi-style jewelry in Flagstaff for some time and then moved elsewhere in Arizona, but continued to supply jewelry to dealers until about 1964.

An Oraibi man, Lewis Lomay (Lomá-yes-va), learned to make silver jewelry from Ambrose Roanhorse at the Indian School in Santa Fe about 1930. He had to quit school during the Depression and went to work in Frank Patania's silver shop in Santa Fe. He smithed there for thirteen years, but now works in construction. He still makes jewelry, often set with turquoise and coral, which has a modern look but retains some Indian character. He has also done some cast work. He continues to enter some of the major exhibitions, and in the 1971 Scottsdale National Indian Arts Exhibition won the First Award in Contemporary Jewelry.

There were other Hopis who were able to do silversmithing with varying degrees of skill prior to 1940. Compared to Zuñi smiths, the number was small and silverwork was a minor craft. But when the figures from about 1940 were checked for the Hopis and the Navajos, the Hopis were not so far behind their close neighbors. Ruth Underhill in *Here Come the Navajo,* 1953 gives the Navajo population for 1940 as 45,000. For that same year, the Hopi population was 3500 according to Laura Thompson and Alice Joseph in their 1944 book, *The Hopi Way.* The Navajos with 600 smiths (Adair: 17) had only about four times as many smiths per capita as the Hopis, with 12 listed silverworkers (Adair: 194). Adair's figures do not include any of the Hopis who were working full time on jewelry away from the Hopi villages, but presumably they also do not include Navajos working away from their reservation. Thus, the proportions stated above would probably be fairly accurate.

Adair suggests that one reason for the smaller number of Hopi silversmiths, compared to Zuñi, was the lack of economic help furnished by nearby traders. At Zuni these traders provided silver and tools on credit and bought the finished jewelry (Adair:178). At Hopi villages the non-Indian traders did nothing to encourage silver-

Plate 12. Necklace and bracelet by Willie Coin, late 1940s. Museum of Northern Arizona.

making and Hopi storekeepers did not have the finances necessary to supply materials and tools on credit.

Another reason for silver remaining a minor craft among the Hopi for years was the competition of other craft work. The women continued their prehistoric art of making pottery and several types of basketry. The men, at certain times, carved kachina dolls and worked on ceremonial objects, as they did at Zuni. But the majority of Hopi men did, and still do, some type of weaving, and any spare hours were devoted to that. This was the source of the *manta* so often mentioned as being traded to the Zuñi. Hopi textiles, coarse white cotton lengths used by the Hopi and other Pueblos for kilts, sashes, and shawls, as well as black wool pieces used for dresses, shirts, and kilts, were much in demand at one time by Indians all

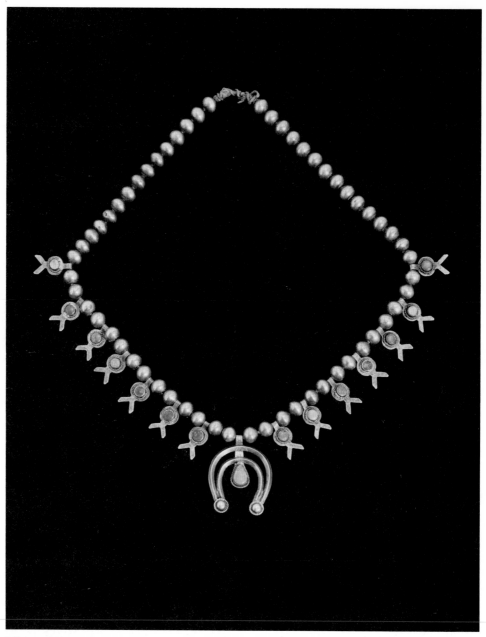

Plate 13. Necklace set with blue and green turquoise by Arthur Masawytewa ca. 1935.

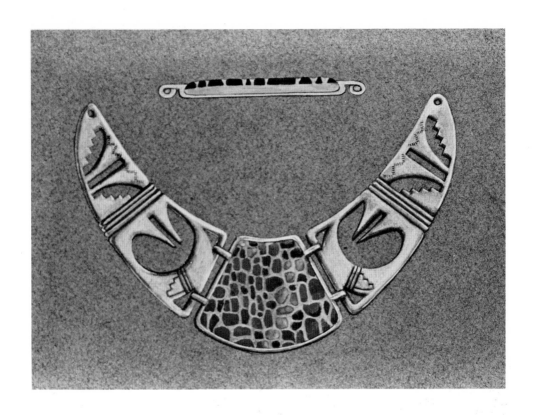

Plate 14. Virgil Hubert silver designs. Museum of Northern Arizona.

31

Plate 15A. Necklace designed and made by Paul Saufkie in 1941.
Museum of Northern Arizona.

Plate 15B. Bracelet crafted by Paul Saufkie in 1941. Museum of Northern Arizona.

over the Southwest, and even today are traded to the Pueblo Indians of the Rio Grande. The Hopi seem to have been the main source of supply, even though the Zuñi and other Pueblo Indians did some weaving. The Navajo men, however, had no such craft to compete with silverworking for their spare time.

One misconception that has arisen about Hopi silver prior to 1940 is that nothing but small articles such as rings, bracelets, and buttons were made. Actually, Adair, from fieldwork done in 1938 and written up in 1940, says that "the little silver that these Hopi make *today* is for the most part small pieces — rings, bracelets, and buttons. Once in a great while a *concha* belt or a bow guard will be made to special order" (Adair:177). Part of the apparent lack of early Hopi jewelry lies in the fact that it was not distinct in style from the Navajo and so was considered as Navajo, once it was removed in distance from its maker. From the pre–1940 silver that is known to be Hopi, I believe that some of the Hopis were excellent silversmiths, able to work with their metal in varying techniques, and that they produced proportionately as many of the larger pieces

33

Plate 15C. Bracelets by Lawrence Saufkie, 1966. Left bracelet is applique. Right is overlay. Museum of Northern Arizona.

such as bow guards, *concha belts,* and necklaces, as their Navajo counterparts. However, there is little indication that they made silver for saddle and bridle decoration.

The *concha* belts were similar in style to those of the Navajo at that time. The bow guards were either hammered or cast, and might show a slight stylistic difference from those made by the Navajo if it were possible to see a number of them together. Necklaces were often made of silver beads with a pendant in the center and eccentric or irregular beads placed around the front of the neck after the fashion of the squash blossom necklace (Plates 7 & 13).

III

Silversmithing Tools

TOOLS WERE A VITAL FACTOR in the adoption of silversmithing by the Hopi. The few tools needed for pottery are easily handmade. Kachina dolls can be carved with only a pocketknife, though a rasp speeds up the work. Baskets take a knife and a punch or an awl. But to work any kind of metal requires a source of forced draft (bellows), an anvil, hammers, and depending upon the type of work to be produced, various tools for holding the metal, for smoothing and shaping the silver, for stamping the designs on the metal, and for heating the solder. The stamped designs found on so much of the southwestern Indian jewelry from the 1900s onward, would not have been possible without very fine files to make the designs on the heads of the dies.

The early Indian artisans became skilled at using simple tools and handling their metal in some ways that the modern smiths cannot duplicate. To make a piece of hammered jewelry, the smith took metal coins and melted them into a small ingot. Then the ingot was hand-hammered and annealed into an even flat sheet, from which the bracelet, pin, *concha,* or object was fashioned. Later on, rollers became available for the smiths to use in flattening their silver. Now silver is bought already formed into sheets, unless it is to be used for casting. The refinements in solder and the acetylene torch with different nozzles have made it easier to do the detailed work characteristic of today's Hopi silversmith, but formerly, a skilled smith was able to do very good work with a blow pipe and bits of silver and flux for solder.

35

The bellows to bring the fire to a hot enough temperature to melt the silver were handmade from buffalo hide by some of the early Navajo and Zuñi smiths. A. F. Whiting, in his *Hopi Crafts Survey* of 1941, found that one of the old Hopi smiths at Hotevilla still had a bellows bought in the early 1900s from the Volz Trading Post. Barrett's photograph of Yellow Light's forge, as well as the picture of Lomá-wunu at Second Mesa, show manufactured bellows.

By 1900 there were trading posts close enough to all the Hopi towns, so that some blacksmithing tools were available to any of the Hopi smiths who could afford to trade for them. Part of these tools could be used for silversmithing, but a silversmith had to be able to fashion some of his own tools or buy them from someone who could make them. Adair tells of a Navajo man, John Six, who was an expert at making dies: "Die-making takes skill and requires a good deal of time. . . . The designs are cut into the ends of the pieces of scrap iron with extremely fine files, and then the dies are tempered by heating and sudden cooling in water, so that the design will hold up under the strain of hammering." He was paid a dollar and a half for a large die, and fifty cents for the smallest size (Adair:103). Lan-ya-de of Zuni told Adair that his Navajo teacher lived with him a year and taught him to make his own dies (Adair:23). Morris Robinson of Bakabi says that he tempered just the outside layer or "shell" of his dies. If they were tempered too hard, they would be brittle and break off when struck by the hammer.

Since Duwá-kuku died in 1956, his tools (Plate 9) could have been obtained any time before then. His anvil is a blacksmith's old "flatter" fastened upright as in plates 1A & 4. The gripping tools include a modern-looking pair of flat-nosed pliers, and a surgical clamp. There is a pair of blacksmith's pincers, and also a bullet mold. Necessary items which are missing are metal shears or scissors, to trim the piece of hammered silver. All of the dies are handmade from old files or from cold chisels (Plate 9A). The female stamp for making beads is from a scrap of iron and had been reworked into a rough chisel end. The files are manufactured, but the ingot mold is made from a piece of sandstone with a high lime content.

36

IV

Important Influences

MUSEUM OF NORTHERN ARIZONA

DR. HAROLD S. COLTON and his wife, Mary-Russell Ferrell Colton, founders of the Museum of Northern Arizona in Flagstaff, worked to encourage the continuation of crafts among the Hopi and to maintain the quality of their work. The Coltons moved to Flagstaff in 1926 from Pennsylvania where Dr. Colton had been a professor of zoology at the University of Pennsylvania since 1909. Mrs. Colton was a recognized artist who had studied at the Philadelphia School of Design for Women. She painted prolifically and worked with the citizens of Flagstaff to foster art shows from other parts of the country and, in turn, have displays of their own art. She especially encouraged the art interests of young people. The Junior Indian Art Show was started for this purpose in 1931 among the Indian youth of northern Arizona.

In 1930 the Coltons established the annual Hopi Craftsman Exhibit at the Museum of Northern Arizona to provide a place for Hopi craft work to be shown and sold, and to furnish an incentive for excellence in the work. They took many trips to the Hopi villages to encourage the production of high quality craft work among the artisans.

At first they concentrated on pottery, basketry, and weaving. Dr. Colton made studies of the firing temperatures of the pottery. When the women had trouble with their black paint rubbing off the pots, the Coltons helped experiment with the varying proportions of ground mineral and plant juice that made an adhesive black. Mrs. Colton also encouraged the women in their use of the old native dyes for their baskets, rather than the aniline dyes from the store. The Museum of Northern Arizona bought indigo, which the Hopis had been using since Spanish times, and furnished it at cost to the weavers who were no longer able to buy it from the traders.

Then in 1938, the Coltons turned their interest to silver work. At about this time, the Bureau of Indian Affairs, under Commissioner John Collier, was sponsoring projects through their Indian Arts and Crafts Board to maintain and improve craft work, including silversmithing, among many Indian groups. Some of these projects had no appreciable long-range success, but others resulted in sustaining crafts that might have been lost completely, while still others raised the quality as well as increasing the output of the crafts. The Navajo Arts and Crafts Guild was a direct result of one of the projects.

Mrs. Colton states some of her thoughts in a letter dated December 5, 1938, to Kenneth E. Chapman, then with the Laboratory of Anthropology, Santa Fe, and a Special Consultant to the Indian Arts and Crafts Board:

> . . . There is only one way to make Hopi silversmithing worthwhile, it must be *different* from any other Indian silversmithing. They must produce *Hopi Silver,* not Navajo, Pueblo, or Zuñi. It must be absolutely unique and of course, the supply will always be limited, therefore, if we can create a worthy product, using *only Hopi design* and advertise it well, we might in time create a small worthwhile market . . .
>
> In order to help the Hopi silversmiths to visualize our idea of Hopi design and to show them how to make use of and adopt pottery, basketry, and textile design to various silver techniques already practiced, we have created a number of plates done in opaque water color on gray paper [Plate 14]. . . . After we start the idea with our designs, we hope that in a short time the idea will take hold and they will no longer be needed. Wherever possible, in making these designs, we have used the stamps already in possession of the smiths . . .
>
> I would like to have your opinion of our plans; of course I realize that all this is going to take a long time as I have acquired much experience after 10 years of work with the Hopi . . .

Virgil Hubert, Assistant Curator of Art at the Museum of Northern Arizona, created the jewelry designs mentioned in Mrs. Colton's

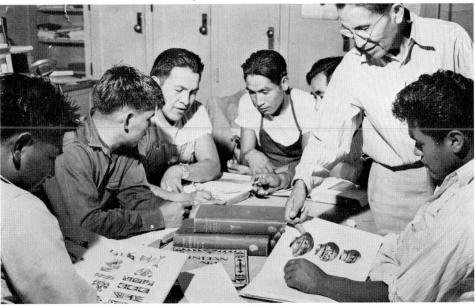

Plate 16. Veterans' class, 1949, studies Hopi designs. *Standing: Fred* Kabotie, Paul Saufkie, Herbert Komayouse, Arthur Yowtewa; *seated:* Bert Puhuyestiwa. Plate 16A. *Left to right:* Arthur Yowytewa, Harold Koruh, Bert Puhuyestiwa, Orville Talayumptewa, Paul Saufkie, Fred Kabotie, Herbert Komayouse. Hopi Cultural Center.

letter. The designs required the use of many silver techniques: filing, stamping, cut-out, and applique. As Hubert worked, he found that the basketry and pottery designs lent themselves especially well to the applique technique, though he hadn't seen any jewelry made in that way. In a personal interview with Hubert, he stated that, contrary to some accounts, he did not make up any of the designs into jewelry.

Eighteen Hopi silversmiths, on the reservation and off — in Arizona, New Mexico, and California — were sent this letter by Mrs. Colton in the spring of 1939:

> In the name of the Museum of Northern Arizona I am writing to all Hopi silversmiths to tell them of our plan to improve Hopi silver and to assist Hopi smiths.
>
> For a number of years, now I have heard Hopi smiths complaining about the low prices which they receive for their work, and of course, it is the same with all the other Indian silversmiths.
>
> This condition, as you know, is caused by the great amount of *machine made, imitation Indian Silver,* which is now being manufactured all over the west. There is so much of this imitation stuff on the market and it can be sold so cheaply, that the Indian smith cannot get a fair price for his genuine *hand made* silver.
>
> The tourist does not know the difference between the *genuine hand made* and the *machine made* and so they are often misled, but they would like to have some guarantee, that the silver which they buy is really hand made.
>
> The government has no law to forbid the making of *imitation Indian silver,* but it has thought out a way to *mark* all hand made Indian silver so that people will know that it is genuine and thus a better price can be charged by the silversmiths for stamped pieces.
>
> I am sending you the papers from the government "Arts and Crafts Board," [Appendix 2] that will tell you just what you have to do to get their mark on your silver work.
>
> The Museum has no connection whatever with the government but feels that it would be an advantage to Hopi smiths to get this stamp. It is hoped that Hopi smiths when using their own designs will place their *personal* marks on their silver also.
>
> I have talked with all the Hopi silversmiths that I can find, both on and off the reservation and explained this to them.

a. tracing
design

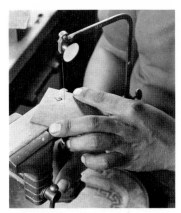

b. sawing
design

c. soldering
design to
backing

d. texturing
background

e. filing to
remove
discoloration

f. buffing

Plate 17. Steps in making overlay jewelry.

41

This is what the government is doing to help, now I am going to give you *the Museum's* idea of what should be done to help the Hopi smiths.

Navajo silver, Hopi and Pueblo silver, is very much alike, most people cannot tell the difference. Hopi silver should be entirely different from all other Indian silver, it should be *Hopi* silver, using only Hopi designs.

Hopi designs are very beautiful and very different from Navajo designs, and they will make beautiful silver and will sell well because the supply will always be limited in quantity.

The Museum proposes to help the Hopi silver smiths in this way. First, we are making a set of designs for silver, using certain Hopi designs in a new way; rings, bracelets, necklaces, etc. An order for one of these pieces and the design from which it is to be made, will be sent to each smith who believes in the idea and wishes to work with us. These pieces will be displayed in the Museum and we will advertise the idea.

We hope that these designs will help the Hopi smiths to understand what we mean by asking them to use one of the Hopi designs, which has not been used for silver before, and *that they will then begin to make their own Hopi designs.*

When I have gotten together a number of silver pieces made with *Hopi design* and *according to the rules of the Arts and Crafts Board,* then the government man will come to the Museum and put the stamp of the "Arts and Crafts Board" on the silver.

This is a very long letter and it is hard to explain, but I am anxious to have you understand.

Let me know if you are interested and wish to have an order to make a piece such as I have described to you. Thanking you, I am

Very sincerely,

MARY-RUSSELL F. COLTON
Curator of Art and Ethnology

The reaction of the smiths who received the letter was varied. Several of them made acceptable pieces for the Hopi Craftsman Show that year. The delicate work necessary to make some of the designs gave a number of the men problems, and a few of the men needed finer tools than they had for the cutting and soldering. One difficulty that arose with the full-time silversmiths as well as their

Plate 18. Bracelets, 1949: *top,* Neilson Honyaktewa; *left,* Douglas Holmes; *right,* Victor Coochwytewa. Museum of Northern Arizona.

employers, was the Indian Arts and Crafts Board's requirements that only slug silver and hand-polished turquoise be used. If not cast, the silver had to be hand-hammered to the desired thickness; no sheet silver was allowed. Mrs. Colton felt this could be resolved by making "premium" pieces which could be stamped by the Arts and Crafts Board and, if necessary for economic reasons, then sheet silver could be used for the regular jewelry that the smiths made. The Hopi smiths felt that all of their handmade jewelry deserved the stamp. At least one trader's position was that the problem about the kind of material to be used would settle itself, and that it was unfortunate to combine it with the introduction of distinctive Hopi designs.

Plate 19. Bracelet, 1949: Dean Siwingyumptewa. The Museum of Northern Arizona.

The points of disagreement would have been resolved in time. Katharine Bartlett of the Museum of Northern Arizona told of one dealer who had not been favorable to the project at first, but in the fall of 1941 came to Flagstaff and spent some time at the Museum discussing the project with the staff (Whiting 4:12).

Paul Saufkie made several of the suggested designs very successfully. A California craft teacher, Glen Lukens, gave Paul several suggestions about the new silver solder that had been developed for use on aircraft, and formulas for oxydizing the background silver in different shades (platinum gray or blue-black). Randall Hon-wiś-i-oma made some good pieces, and Gene Nuvá-hoi-oma, Pierce Kewań-wy-tewa, and Washington Talaý-ump-tewa also completed suitable pieces. Saufkie (Plates 15A & B) and Randall Hon-wiś-i-oma were working on designs of their own in a similar style in 1941 (Whiting 4:7) and Morris Talá-wy-tewa (Robinson) had become interested by December of 1941 (Whiting 4:12).

In another letter to Kenneth Chapman, Mrs. Colton says, "Some very nice pieces are beginning to come in now and I think that in a few years we may be able to make considerable impression."

However, the Coltons did not have the few years needed. After the Pearl Harbor attack in 1941, many aspects of business and daily life

Plate 20. Copper bowl by Tom Humiyestiwa, 1949. Museum of Northern Arizona.

45

Plate 21. Bracelets, 1949: *from top,* Herbert Komayouse, Paul Saufkie, Orville Talayumptewa, Orville Talyumptewa. Museum of Northern Arizona.

Plate 22. Bracelet, 1949: by Lavern Siwiyumptewa. Museum of Northern Arizona.

were quickly changed. The Hopi in the villages were more insulated against these changes than the average American. However, they were still affected — their eligible men joined the armed forces or were imprisoned as conscientious objectors; others did war work of various kinds. Villagers at home had to do the extra work of those taken away. There were shortages of all kinds: rationing of shoes, sugar, gasoline, meat, butter, tires. No metal of any kind was available. The Museum of Northern Arizona was shorthanded and lacked gasoline, but was able to make one collecting trip and hold a Hopi Craftsman Show in 1942. Then no more were held until the summer of 1947. During those five years it had been impossible to continue the silver project.

VETERANS' SILVERSMITHING CLASSES: 1947–1951

In the late summer of 1946, as reported in the August 22 issue of the *Arizona Sun,* Fred Kabotie and other villagers got together an exhibit of Hopi crafts to be shown during the Snake Dance at Shungopavi. Willard Beatty, Director of Indian Education, who knew of the previous encouragement of the craftsmen by the Museum of Northern Arizona, attended the exhibit. The next day he met with Kabotie and Paul Saufkie and arranged for the G.I. training program for veterans to sponsor an eighteen-month silversmithing course for Hopi servicemen. This program paid for the cost of the training and

47

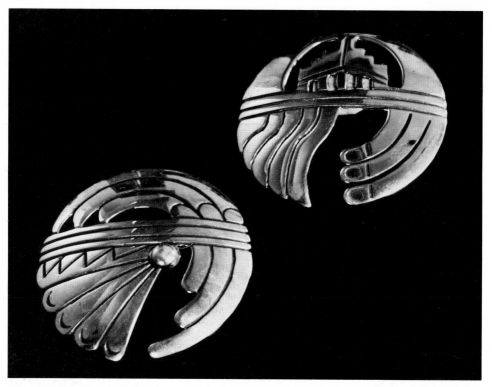

Plate 23. Pins, 1949: by Travis Yaiva and Herbert Komayouse. Museum of Northern Arizona.

provided the necessary tools, as well as paying living expenses for the veteran and his family.

The classes were started in February of 1947. Paul Saufkie was hired as the technical instructor and Fred Kabotie, along with his job as an art teacher at Hopi High School in New Oraibi, was the design instructor. The classes met at Hopi High School (Plate 16), and later were moved to a Quonset hut nearby. While the designs suggested by the Museum of Northern Arizona were used by the trainees, there was also a wealth of new designs taken from the large variety available in Hopi culture. In addition the book of Mimbres designs prepared by Fred Kabotie under a Guggenheim fellowship, provided further inspiration.

Plate 24. Necklace, pin, and ring by Vernon Talas, 1949. Museum of Northern Arizona.

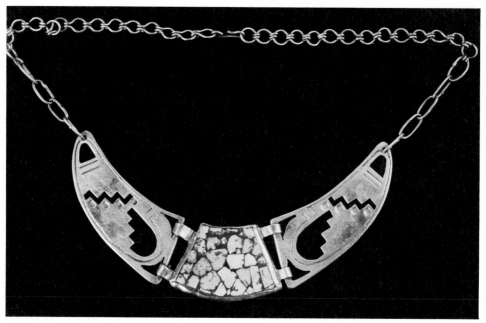

Plate 25. Necklace by Valjean Joshevema, 1949. Museum of Northern Arizona.

The silver was worked with many techniques but one was developed that is now thought of as especially Hopi. Some of the Museum of Northern Arizona designs had been formed by applique, in which a design is cut out and put on a base (Plate 15 *left*). While this was used somewhat, soon "the piece that was left" (Plate 15 *right*) became the design, originating the jewelry technique so widely used now, and called "overlay."

SILVER OVERLAY TECHNIQUE

Overlay, as used in Hopi silverwork, is basically a piece of silver with a design cut out of it — a negative design. An everyday example of this would be the hole left in a piece of dough by a cookie cutter: if one is making star-shaped cookies, a star-shaped hole remains in the dough that is left. This is the principle of the overlay technique — the silver that is left after the design has been cut out of it,

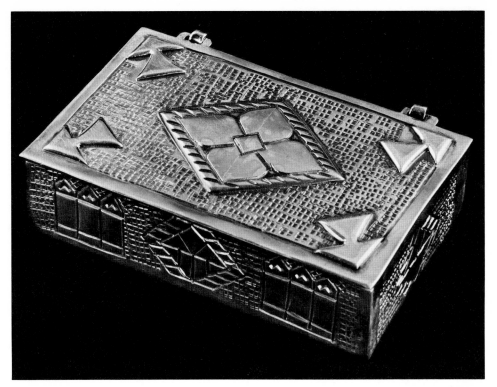

Plate 26. Box by Clarence Lomayestewa, 1949. Museum of Northern Arizona.

is the part which is used. This piece is soldered onto a sheet of plain silver and the inside of the design oxidized to show up black against the polished silver.

The smiths work from sheet silver and trace their designs from metal templates they have already cut out (Plate 17a). A hole is punched in the part to be cut out, and a tiny saw blade is inserted. Then the design is carefully sawed out, the most painstaking step in the whole process (Plate 17b). The lines must be steady and smooth, for no correction of them is possible. After the design piece is sawed, it is well coated with a flux, as is the plain piece of silver. The one is laid on top of the other and the two are heated to a red glow with an acetylene torch. Wire solder is melted along the edge and flows between the two pieces, firmly soldering them together (Plate 17c).

After the piece of silver is cooled, the matting or texturing of the design is done. Tiny chisels with the ends shaped in a straight line, curved, or wedge-shaped, are used with a rawhide hammer. The chisel marks are placed to follow the shape of the design (Plate 17d). At this time the bottom piece of silver must be trimmed and the whole piece hammered to its finished shape, whether it is a bracelet, a pendant with a soft swell to it, or the *conchas* of a belt curved to fit around the waist. Then any findings necessary, such as earring and cuff link fastenings, the pin for a pendant, or the loop for a belt buckle are soldered on.

The piece is blanched in acid to remove any discolorations, especially from the heating. Then liver of sulphur, in some form, is applied to the interior of the design to oxidize (darken) it. This dark oxidized area is "set" by immersing the piece in boiling water. The jewelry is filed and polished with emery paper to remove discoloration and roughness (Plate 17e). This is a step that must be done carefully and thoroughly to ensure a well-finished piece. It is then cleaned with ammonia water, after which it is buffed and polished and ready for sale (Plate 17f).

The method of making this style of jewelry has not changed appreciably in twenty years, except for the present consistent use of matting in the design. In 1949 it was seldom done (Plate 18) though texturing was used as a major part of the design (Plate 19).

The students worked with copper for practice because it was less expensive, and produced a few pieces for sale (Plate 20). After the Hopi Guild had been established, its 1950 catalog listed silver jewelry with copper inlay as being available through orders (though Fred Kabotie said it was difficult to make because of the difference in the melting points of the metals). J. H. McGibbeny's article in the July 1950 *Arizona Highways* shows hollowware made with a partial copper exterior. But apparently very few of these mixed copper and silver items were made.

Some of the finished pieces from the veterans' silver class were

Plate 27. Cast buckle set with turquoise, Paul Saufkie, 1949. Museum of Northern Arizona.

Plate 28. Fred Kabotie in the Hopi Silvercraft Cooperative Guild sales-room, 1972.

displayed and sold at the Indian Craft Shop of the Department of Interior, Washington, D.C., in December 1948. The first complete display of the work was offered for sale in July 1949 at the Hopi Craftsman Exhibit of the Museum of Northern Arizona.

The inspiration of the individual craftsmen and the way they used their designs resulted in a diversity of jewelry styles. There were numerous examples of the overlay technique (Plate 21). Others used various textures (Plates 19 & 22) or *repoussé* (see Cover) to obtain pleasing effects. Abstract forms were used in cut-out styles (Plates 23, 24 & 25), while the original die and chisel technique was used for beautiful new pieces (Plate 26), as was cast work (Plate 27). A fair amount of turquoise was featured, sometimes as an element of the design.

The first veterans' class graduated in 1949. The subsistence payments to the men stopped at graduation, and they lacked any means of getting more silver to make into jewelry.

HOPI SILVERCRAFT COOPERATIVE GUILD

With the help and encouragement of the Indian Arts and Crafts Board and the Hopi Government Agency, the Hopi Silvercraft Guild was formed in 1949. Its purpose was stated: "To produce, purchase, and sell handcrafts and to operate related activities." Through this

Plate 29. Silver bowl, 1972, and double-faced pendant, 1965, by Bernard Dawahoya. Bracelet by Harry Sakyesva, about 1962, collection of Mrs. Tom Pollock.

55

Plate 30. 1972. Belt by Hubert Yowytewa. Barrette by Patrick Lomawaima. Pendant necklace, two bracelets, *far right,* and *lower left,* by
Victor Coochwytewa. Bolo tie by Franklin Namingha, center bracelet
by Phillip Honani, ring by Dalton Taylor.

56

Plate 31. 1972. Bracelets, *top, lower right,* and *lower left,* by Glenn Lucas. Belt buckles, *right* and *left,* and center pendant, Eldon James. Oval belt buckles, *right* and *left,* Weaver Selina. *Lower center,* double-faced pendant, 1967, by Phillip Honani. Museum of Northern Arizona.

Plate 32. Paul Saufkie at Second
Mesa, 1972.

organization the smiths were able to borrow $5000 from the government to purchase supplies and equipment. The Guild members continued to work in part of the Quonset hut and after the second class had graduated on January 1, 1951, they were able to use the whole building. Fred Kabotie was elected secretary-treasurer and served in that position until he was transferred by the government from Indian Education to work under the Indian Arts and Crafts Board as manager of the Guild. His wife, Alice, was then elected secretary-treasurer, and both have continued to serve the Guild for many years. In 1971 Kabotie retired as manager, but is still active in the Guild (Plate 28).

In 1962 ground was broken for a new Guild building a mile northwest of the entrance to Shungopavi. There was some controversy at first about this use of the land. Mishongnovi and Shipaulovi villages laid claim to the land, as did Shungopavi. The land was outside clan holdings but was under the jurisdiction of Shungopavi because it was a kachina trail from a sacred spring to the village. The new building was erected without incident and the Hopi Cultural Center and Motel were built nearby in 1971. There is display and sales space in the Guild building as well as working space.

The relationship of the silversmiths to the Guild takes various forms. A few of the men, mostly the older ones who have been away, have no connection with the organization. Others have worked for

Plate 33A. Buckle, Gracilda Saufkie, 1966. Marc Gaede Photograph.

it full time almost from the start. These men depend upon their jewelry sales or salaries received from the Guild for their total income. Other smiths work at their homes for their cash income, with or without ties to the Guild. Then there are various craftsmen who work part-time at silver, a little or a lot, and they may work for the Guild or independently. The Guild supplies the silver for all jewelry made under its auspices and these pieces are marketed by the Guild rather than by the individual craftsmen. However, the pieces are identified and sold as each smith's own work. The jewelry does not have to be made in the Guild shop.

During the more than twenty years of its existence, the Guild has been very beneficial to the Hopi smiths by providing a central workshop and a stable marketing outlet. Without it, the benefits of the veterans' classes would not have had such lasting effects.

PRIVATE ENTERPRISE: HOPICRAFTS SHOP

In 1961 a silver shop was opened at New Oraibi by two brothers, Wayne and Emory Seká-quap-tewa. They had learned silverwork in Phoenix from an excellent smith, Harry Sak-yeś-va (Plate 29), who was in ill health and lived with them while Wayne was working for a radio station. The Seká-quap-tewa brothers started a business, Hopi Enterprise, in Phoenix and hired another brother and Bernard Dawá-hoya and Eldon James as silversmiths. Peter Shelton, Jr. was hired as a designer. The business was moved to New Oraibi and the name was shortly changed to Hopicrafts. (Note: The names of *Hopicrafts,* a private business, and the *Hopi Silvercraft Guild* are easily confused. To avoid this, I attempt to emphasize *Guild* when I am talking of that organization.) The Hopicrafts salesroom was moved in 1971 to the new Cultural Center at Shungopavi, though the workshop remains at New Oraibi.

The jewelry produced by the business was especially well-made, with close attention paid to even sawing, careful filing, and fine polishing. The smallest details of each piece, such as the silver tips on the braid of a bolo tie, were as carefully made as the rest of the article. The competition of Hopicrafts caused a general upgrading of the quality of all the Hopi jewelry, which in some instances had been poorly finished and made of too light a weight of silver, as well as becoming stereotyped in design. The Hopi overlay of today shows the influence of designer Peter Shelton, Jr. and others from Hopicrafts. The use of Hohokam figures, animal and human figures in motion, the elaborate detailing, all are a result of Hopicrafts design.

Two other innovations were the result of the Oraibi business. From the beginning the Seká-quap-tewas used texturing in the matte black background of all their jewelry. While it had been used slightly before, it now became a basic part of the design, usually following the pattern of the overlay (Plate 29). The attractive appearance, as well as the fact that the rough surface retains the blackening agent much better, has resulted in its widespread use by many Hopi silversmiths today. Hopicrafts also gives the final polish to the silver with steel wool, which gives it a satin rather than a bright finish.

The establishment of Hopicrafts caused hard feelings for a time. This was intensified by the fact that some of the pieces of jewelry were not crafted individually but rather were made by several smiths doing the work on each piece, with each man performing one set operation. However, Hopicrafts' influence has resulted in an im-

Plate 33B. Bolo tie, 1970, Lawrence Saufkie.

provement in the quality of jewelry produced by all the smiths, even though at times the designs have become increasingly baroque.

CHANGES IN HOPI CULTURAL LIFE

At present there are only two full-time silversmiths working away from the Hopi villages, compared with the 1930s when there were at least six. This is partly the result of better roads, which not only bring more tourists to the Hopi country, but also make it easy for the silversmiths to take their finished work to Phoenix, Gallup, Albuquerque, and cities in California. The better roads also permit more regular mail service, which facilitates orders.

There have been many changes in the lives of Hopi people since 1900 in addition to better roads, just as there have been for all Americans. The surprising thing is that after three-quarters of a century of world-wide change and increasing communication with non-Indians, the Hopis have kept a great part of their old culture. Numerous Hopis live all over the United States, but many have found jobs close enough to the villages so that they can attend the important rituals of their people. These people often move back to Hopi when they retire and some of them plant fields that had lain fallow while they were away.

The villagers live mainly on food bought at the store, but enough corn is raised to provide everyone with blue corn flour for the stacks of *piki* bread each family still makes. White Hopi corn is available either from their own fields or by purchase from other Hopi growers so that each household can serve the traditional *nukwivi,* or hominy stew, to everyone who visits during a kachina dance.

The women may use corn grinders driven by electricity or turned by hand, but others grind their *piki* flour on a grinding stone or *metate.* Girls from Shungopavi still grind corn this way for four days as part of a ritual in a Hopi adolescent ceremony. Much of the cooking is a successful adaptation of the new combined with the old — coarse shallow yucca baskets are used as colanders alongside electric skillets. Hopi pottery is seldom used for cooking food, though the *piki* batter is mixed in a native bowl.

Plate 34. Charles Loloma. Silver hair clip, 1972. Single turquoise pendant earring, 1967; silver cast ring, 1964. Roxine Phillippi Collection. Gold ring set with turquoise; gold bracelet with emeralds and interior inlaid with turquoise mosaic; carved jade pendant; silver bracelet set with ivory, ironwood, and coral, all made in 1972. Cast corn maiden, ironwood buckle, and cast pin, 1968. Museum of Northern Arizona.

Water now flows on top of First Mesa and Shungopavi! Where the women used to walk down to the spring each day to carry up all the water for a household, they can now walk over to a faucet and fill their buckets. After some of the springs dried up and people did not want to carry water up the steep trails, owners of pickup trucks would haul water from distant windmills, charging a dollar for fifty gallons. But now all of First Mesa has water from a tank at Hano (it is piped to the houses at Polacca). Shungopavi has a good well and a large storage tank, New Oraibi has water piped to the houses, and Hotevilla, Bakabi, and Moencopi have water taps placed in the villages.

Silversmiths at Shungopavi and all of First Mesa except Walpi now have electricity available to them, and of course both the Guild shop and Hopicrafts have electricity. It is available on the outskirts of Hotevilla but is not permitted in the village, so smiths living there must use hand-turned or gasoline-powered buffing wheels.

High school-age children must now go at least as far as Phoenix to the Indian School there, though a number also go to Sherman Institute in Riverside, California, and Haskell Institute in Kansas. Some young people, especially from Christian families, stay in private homes in California and Utah while they attend school. Those who have shown marked artistic ability are chosen to attend the Institute of American Indian Arts at Santa Fe.

There is talk of starting the Hopi High School again so that a number of children in their teens will be able to remain with their parents and attend school. At Tuba City, Arizona a large school is being built which will serve jointly as a boarding school for Navajo children and a day school for all young people who live nearby, including the residents of Moencopi.

Jobs held by village residents are often with the government. Many of the old people live on what they raise in their fields, plus a state old-age payment or a social security check. Both men and women work at the five Hopi grade schools, generally as maintenance men, cooks, and aides, though one principal is a Hopi and there are several Hopi teachers. There is other work with the highway de-

Plate 35. Three-dimensional pin crafted by Richard Kagenvema, 1968. Museum of Northern Arizona.

partment, Hopi police, the government hospital and BIA offices at Keams Canyon, and the Tribal offices at New Oraibi. Now a government housing project employs Indian construction workers. They built a number of houses at Hopi, and then moved on to the Apache reservation for fifteen months of work, taking their families with them.

Men who live in towns close enough to come home easily for kachina and other ceremonies work at all manner of jobs. Many are employed by the United States Forest Service, permanently or part-time, and others work in the logging industry. Most employers give their Hopi workers time off to attend any important rituals that take longer than a weekend. But the burden of maintaining daily ritual tasks falls necessarily upon the men who are residents of the villages.

Ritual life is still very important for the majority of Hopis, though there are some so Christianized that they avoid contact with any of the ceremonials. Others practice both Hopi and Christian religions. The full ritual calendar has been lost at some villages, so not all the ceremonies are performed. Kachina dances continue to be numerous and the widely-known though less important Snake Dance is still performed along with other non-kachina dances. In 1972 Mishongnovi closed all ceremonials to non-Hopis. Normally anyone who "has a good heart" has been welcome to attend the dances and add their prayers to those of the Hopis for well-being throughout the world.

V

Contemporary Silversmiths

FOR MEN who want to stay at the villages, have artistic talent, and like to work with their hands, silversmithing provides an excellent occupation. The market for Indian jewelry has become so great that the demand exceeds the supply, though whether this will be a temporary fashion remains to be seen. A silversmith can set his own working hours so that he may tend his fields and take part in rituals whenever necessary. This lack of dependence upon the clock does make for irregular delivery of jewelry or repairs and should be realized by anyone dealing with the smiths. Actually, full-time silversmithing is an occupation that allows the men to participate fully in the ceremonial calendar, as was possible in former times when all the men were farmers.

Not all the men who attended the veterans' classes graduated, and some who did, made no jewelry afterward. Others have kept their tools and hope to get back to it. An Oraibi man had done nothing for years, but recently has made some bow guards, and hopes to continue to do more. Several of the men have made small amounts of jewelry all along, as the occasion demanded. Others have worked steadily at the Guild. Wallie Seká-yump-tewa made jewery for many years as well as helping with the Guild salesroom. Now that his eyes are giving him difficulty, he does repair work and spends the rest of the time in the many other jobs involved with jewelry sales.

Victor Cooch-wý-tewa has continued to make a large quantity of jewelry (Plate 30). He worked with Paul Saufkie before World War II, but attended the veterans' classes also. He is affiliated with the

Guild, but has marketed his silver individually as well, even selling it to Hopicrafts for re-sale. In the 1950s he made silver overlay buckles and tooled leather belts in a matching design. These were unusual and very handsome. He is one of the religious society leaders at Shungopavi and both he and his wife take an active part in the ceremonies. He has been employed by the highway department while continuing to do silverwork. Victor still makes *concha* belts, large and small, usually on order.

Marshall Jenkins' work in silver jewelry is a good example of what often happens with all types of Hopi crafts. While at school in Albuquerque, he learned silversmithing by helping the noted teacher Chester Yellowhair. However, he made very little jewelry until he was forced into retirement by a back ailment when he was in his forties. He then made a number of pieces of jewelry. Now he is working for one of the Hopi schools and doesn't have much time for silverwork.

Lawrence and Gracilda Saufkie (Plate 33A & B) are full-time silversmiths. As a boy, Lawrence would sneak in and use the tools of his father, Paul Saufkie. When Paul caught him at it, he said he would teach him. Lawrence worked in his teens making, among other things, copper buttons which he sold, six for a dollar and a half. After he married he started silverwork again. His wife, the former Gracilda Nuvumsa, helped him and gradually learned the whole process. She made silver for several years before using her own mark. Lawrence often used the bears and bear paws of his clan as designs for his jewelry (Plate 15C). The Saufkies want to sell at the Cultural Center, but have not been able to get a sufficient backlog of jewelry to stock a shop. They, as well as Bernard Dawá-hoya, exhibit at the Gallup Ceremonial and similar events and this, coupled with their regular sales outlets, keeps their stock depleted.

Bernard Dawá-hoya (Little Sun) and Eldon James have both become independent smiths. They worked originally for the Seká-quaptewa brothers in Phoenix and Oraibi. Bernard first learned smithing from his uncle, Sidney Secá-kuku, and another relative, Washington Talay-ump-tewa. He was at the Guild for a short while before going

67

to Hopicrafts, where he later helped instruct new smiths. He now has a workshop at Shungopavi and a sales shop at the Hopi Cultural Center where his jewelry shows the same elegance of finish it had when he worked at Hopicrafts. Bernard makes all form of jewelry and often makes other objects, especially round boxes and bowls (Plate 30).

Eldon James, a native of Hotevilla, has a workshop at his wife's house at Shungopavi and delivers his finished jewelry to Indian craft stores in Arizona. He specializes in jewelry which is very well-finished (Plate 31), but makes no hollowware.

Preston Mo-nong̈-ye was adopted by a Hopi family when he was a small child and takes part in the Hopi religious ceremonies at Hotevilla. He originally learned silversmithing from a relative, Gene Nuvá-hoi-oma, in the late thirties, and first made jewelry in the style of that period. He became very proficient in the overlay technique, but now works in a modern or "new Indian" style using both silver and gold in many variations. He achieves a flamboyancy in his jewelry by the use of inlays of shell, many varieties of stones, and fine quality turquoise. At the same time, other jewelry will be made by intricate casting, often in combination with overlay, to obtain subtle pieces which may be set off by only one or two stones (frontispiece). He has won numerous awards in every major exhibition in recent years.

Charles Lóloma is a noted craftsman from Hotevilla, who has worked in ceramics as well as silver. He studied ceramics at Alfred University, New York, and taught at the Institute of American Indian Arts at Santa Fe from 1962 to 1964. He painted murals for the San Francisco Exposition in 1939 under the direction of Rene d' Harnoncourt of the Indian Arts and Crafts Board. While living at Shungopavi in 1950 and teaching under a Whitney Foundation Fellowship, he became interested in silverwork. Later in Phoenix he often sought the advice and criticism of Fred Sharp, Bob Winston, and Morris Robinson. At first he did only cast work but now at his workshop in Hotevilla he employs many different techniques in both silver and gold. He uses a variety of stones as well as wood and ivory in combination with the silver and gold. While his work is exotic, his designs are taken from Hopi objects, surroundings, and traditions (Plate 34). His work has been featured in exhibits throughout this country and in Europe.

The jewelry of Charles Lóloma and Preston Mo-nong-ye has an individual style, now distinctly removed from the silverwork made by most Hopi smiths. Preston Mo-nong-ye prefers to class it, along with jewelry made by several other Indians, as "new Indian" (*Arizona Highways,* June 1972).

VI

Today's Hopi Silver Jewelry

TRADITIONAL HOPI SILVER JEWELRY of today is distinctive from other Indian jewelry. The smiths themselves show many individual styles, some easy to see and others very subtle. The differences range from the work of Richard Ka-geń-vema (pronounced Ka-chiń-vema) of the original veterans' classes, who uses cut-out designs which are put together to form three-dimensional pieces (Plate 35), to that of Leroy Kewań-yama which features irregular shapes as a base, rather than symmetrical forms (Plate 36). Both Ted Wadsworth and Victor Cooch-wý-tewa use coral and turquoise more frequently than other smiths. Hopicrafts uses no stones at all, and most other smiths are using very little turquoise, especially since today it is scarce and high priced. Smiths can often be recognized by their frequent use of characteristic designs or by the way in which design and space are interwoven.

There is an infinite variety of design in the traditions of Hopi culture. This culture employs a great wealth of symbols which are visible signs of ideas. These are not a form of writing but rather, both for sacred and secular use, to express an association or quality. Therefore, a woman may depict a field and clouds with rain falling, in graphic form, on a coiled basket. At the same time the long fringe hanging down from the white wedding belt also depicts rain, which brings fertility. This, in turn, symbolizes a fruitful marriage to provide more Hopi people to follow in the ways of the kachinas and harvest abundantly from the land. From their daily lives the people are accustomed to seeing stylization of objects. Their

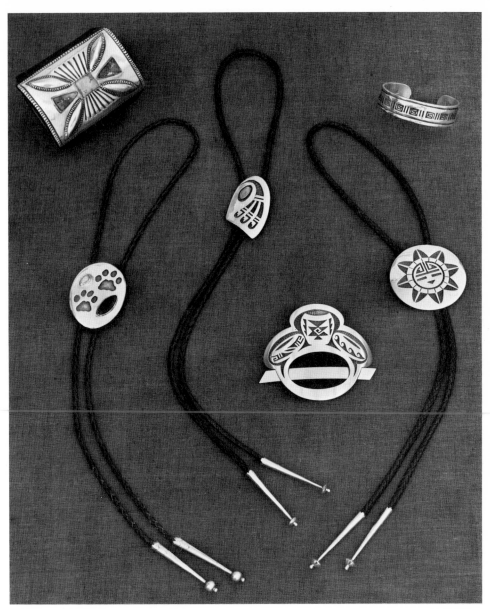

Plate 36. Bow guard and hand-hammered bracelet, Paul Saufkie, 1972. *Left,* bolo tie, Willie Coin, 1971. *Center,* bolo tie, Leroy Kewan-yama, 1972. *Right,* bolo tie, Billie Ray Hawee, 1972. Barrette, Hubert Yowytewa, 1972.

71

craftwork has long made use of these stylizations, so that transferring them to silverwork did not have inherent problems, once they grasped the idea of relying completely upon their own background rather than depending upon outside sources. Contrary to some Indian craft work which does depict a specific idea or story, most Hopi silverwork is designed for its appearance. Many of the elements may represent a specific thing; for instance: warrior marks [symbol] ; hair whorl [symbol] ; an infinite variety of clouds and precipitation (as may be seen in the hallmarks) [symbol] ; feathers [symbol] ; whirlwind [symbol] ; but they are actually put together to form a pleasing effect. At other times a silversmith may design a piece which has a personal meaning or thought in it.

In addition to the voluminous number of stylized symbols, some prehistoric Mimbres designs have been incorporated into the jewelry, and a number of the early Hohokam figures from central Arizona are now used along with petroglyphs from northern Arizona. The designs on prehistoric Anasazi potsherds in the vicinity of the villages have also been used extensively. Katharine Bartlett of the Museum of Northern Arizona reports that in the 1950s it was possible to name the pottery type of the sherds used for the silver designs, so similar were the designs to the broken pots. Add to all of these sources the wealth of kachina figures, and it becomes apparent that there is a vast resource of design material from which the Hopi silversmiths may draw. The styles can range from complete realism, as in the depiction of a kachina, to a very simple, completely stylized design. None of the many designs are traditional for use on silver, as they are on basketry, weaving, and other crafts. Thus the design on any piece of silver jewelry eventually depends upon the inspiration and artistic skill of the individual smith.

One jewelry technique which has been carried from prehistoric times to the present is the use of turquoise mosaic. Examples of this work inlaid in shell, wood, and even on basketry have been found during excavation of early archaeological sites and the Hopi have

Plate 37. Bracelets, *upper center* and *lower right,* Billie Ray Hawee. *Lower left,* bracelet, McBride Lomayestewa. Two central left bracelets, Hubert Yowytewa. Link belt, Phillip Honani.

continued to use it during historic times. In 1938 Virgil Hubert drew a necklace using mosaic (Plate 14), and necklaces of that type were made in the 1940s (Plates 12 & 25). At the same time that some smiths were adapting the turquoise mosaic to their silver jewelry, other men continued to make jewelry in the ancient way, with the mosaic inlaid in wood. In 1972 Charles Lóloma incorporated mosaic in a unique way, using it to line the back of one of his modern gold bracelets (Plate 34).

Forms of Hopi jewelry change much more readily than designs. This is due to economic pressures, especially the whims of the buying public, whether the Hopi themselves, who were the major buyers of the early 1900s, or the present-day collectors. Pieces made in the 1930s by commercial smiths ranged from bowls and candlesticks to all types of jewelry, and the same is true today. Silver styles change along with dress and home decorating fashions. Choker-type necklaces (Plates 12 & 25) were common in the 1940s and 1950s but are seldom made now. At present, a large number of pendants and pendant necklaces (Plates 29 & 30), are made. Earrings readily follow fashion, being button-type or pendant, large or small, or even a dramatic single! (Plate 34). A piece which has come into wide fashion all over the Southwest is the *bolo* tie, which is now worn by many men, Indian as well as non-Indian, in place of the conventional tie. The Hopi make many *bolos* for sale, using the same type of design they put on other pieces.

There are few *concha* belts being made by Hopi silversmiths now, though they do make up belts from various kinds of medallions (Plates 30 & 37). A number of bow guards are still being made, almost entirely for Hopi use. A man who does very little smithing may make up one of these *maponi* for his relatives, himself, or to sell to other Hopis. The bow guards are worn in many kachina dances, as well as the butterfly, buffalo, and other non-kachina ceremonies, so they are in constant demand. Bracelets worn by the dancers are usually Navajo or Zuni, set with much turquoise, and the necklaces are of nugget turquoise or of coral.

The number of active silversmiths in a given year is variable. The important thing is that the craft is still vigorous (I must state that this is being written during a time of extremely brisk sales of all Indian crafts) and barring unforseen events, will probably continue for some time, even more so than the traditional crafts which depend to a greater degree on Hopi culture. Silversmithing still provides an ideal occupation for Hopi men and women who want to remain at the Hopi villages. It allows them to participate fully in Hopi life, including the farming that is so basic to their culture, and yet supplies the cash income necessary for the modern Hopi family.

Let us hope that Hopi silversmiths will preserve and take inspiration from their rich cultural traditions, and that they will, at the same time, give free expression to their individual talents and perceptions. This combination should continue to produce a vital and distinctive art form.

VII

Hopi Silver Hallmarks

MUCH OF THE HOPI SILVER made now is stamped on the back with the smith's personal symbol. Silver hallmarks became widely used on Hopi silver during the veterans' classes in 1949. A few of the older smiths marked their silver in the 1930s. It will be noted that Mrs. Colton also urged them to do this, in her letter on page 40. In 1938 the Indian Arts and Crafts Board authorized a stamp "U. S. Hopi" though it is doubtful that many items were marked with it. Silver produced under Hopi Guild auspices is marked with its insignia, the sun symbol, as well as with the individual smith's mark. Since ties with the Guild are not constant, a man may buy silver himself and turn out a number of pieces which he will market at the same time that he is working for the Guild. Thus in the same time period one may buy jewelry with both the Guild mark and the smith's stamp, as well as pieces with only the smith's mark.

Workers for Hopicrafts formerly marked their silver with the firm's symbol only, with the exception of a few special pieces. Now some of the smiths are stamping their own initials on the Hopicrafts pieces regularly.

In the majority of instances, the marks used by the silversmiths are symbols of their clans. In theory a clan is a group of people who trace their descent from a common ancestor. Among the Hopis, this line is carried through the women, so all the children belong to their mother's clan. Wiser heads than I have tried to sort out Hopi clans and clan membership. In the succeeding list I have simply stated the clan that was given me by the smith himself or another Hopi.

Many clans "go together." In these instances a symbol from any one of them is considered one's own clan symbol. Groups that are found in this list are: Sun, Sun's Forehead, and Eagle; Waterhouse (*Patki*) and Young Corn (*Pikyas*); Rabbit and Tobacco; Badger and Butterfly; Snake and Lizard; Bear, Strap, and Spider (Antelope also goes with this group); Snow and Fog; Kachina and Parrot.

In at least one known instance, the father's clan symbol was used. Other hallmarks were chosen for no obvious reason, since a smith could pick whichever mark he wished. In one instance at least, a hallmark was reused — Vernon Mansfield is now using Willard Nuvá-yauoma's feather mark, but he doubles it.

Simply because a person is listed does not mean that he is, or was, a professional silversmith. I have tried to indicate, whenever possible, the extent of a smith's work. Even though a Hopi did no more work than that done in his veterans' classes, it is likely that pieces of his work are in the hands of the public. The class work was sold at the Indian Arts and Crafts Board Exhibit in Washington, D.C., the Hopi Craftsman Shows of the Museum of Northern Arizona, the Arizona State Fair in Phoenix, and at the Hopi Silver-craft Guild, when it was established. After the veterans' classes ended, new smiths learned their trade by working at the Hopi Guild, unless it is otherwise noted on the list.

The smiths are listed in approximate chronological order, based on available information. Note that there are no hallmarks listed for many of the early smiths, since the practice did not begin until the 1930s. For brevity Hopi names are written in their traditional form, without hyphen or accents. Many of the smiths are known by several names, not including nicknames. The Hopis originally had no system of surnames, but were given new names to replace the old upon important occasions in their lives. Some of the names on the list are derived from this custom. Others have resulted from the children being given English names at school which were used with their Indian names, and still others are the gradual development of a family name. Paul Andrew was the son of Andrew. He later used one of his Hopi names, Saufkie, as a last name and now all his children use that as a last name. Most of the young people today have one set of names, including a given English name and their father's "last" name, that they use officially. However, they are still given, and keep, personal Hopi names.

Many smiths have several villages listed under their residence. Among the Hopi a man customarily goes to live at his wife's home. Thus, normally, if he marries a woman from another village, he moves to his wife's village and becomes a resident there.

Several things are made apparent by the list of smiths. Among the men who took silversmithing under the G.I. Bill, less than half continued to work. However, this percentage may compare favorably with the results of any of the other veterans' training programs.

Sadder to note is the large number of silversmiths who have been killed. This may well reflect the high accident rate among the Hopi as a whole. Another striking figure is the number of smiths who became blind or had to quit work because of poor eyesight. Again, the Hopi as a group are subject to eye maladies. However, John Adair in his discussion of Navajo silversmiths calls eyestrain "the occupational disease of silversmithing." He also said that a smith could plan to do accurate work for only about twenty years before his eyes grew too weak to do silversmithing (Adair:104). While many of the smiths working today have electric lights to see by, they also use acetylene torches a great deal, without any eye protection. Whether this actually contributes to deteriorating eyesight or not, the smiths feel it does. Whatever the causes, the list does show that a common reason for discontinuing silverwork is failing eyesight.

Hallmarks

THE SMALL BOXES NEXT TO THE VARIOUS MARKS INDICATE
ACTUAL SIZE OF MARK.

SILVERSMITH	CLAN	VILLAGE	BEGAN SILVER WORK	WORKED SILVER UNTIL	HALLMARK
Sikyatala	Mustard	Sichomovi	ca.1890	d. after 1916	No Mark
Duwakuku	Mustard	Sichomovi	pre-1900	d.1956	No Mark
(Also: Tuwakuku) Born around 1865. Assume he began silverwork before 1900. Father of Hano potter, Garnet Pavatea.					
Andrew Humiquaptewa	Bluebird	Shungopavi	pre-1900	d. ca. 1962	No Mark
A blacksmith who taught himself to make silver. Made brass objects before he worked silver. After the railroad reached Williams, Arizona (1882), took silver bracelets to the Havasupai and traded for buckskins.					
Tawanimptewa	Water-house	Shungopavi	ca.1900	ca.1930 d.1953	No Mark
(Also: Tewaneptewa; Nickname: Sitakpu) Worked at Grand Canyon.					
Tawahongniwa	Bear	Shungopavi	pre-1900	d.1920	No Mark
Joshua Homiyesva	Sun	Shungopavi	ca.1900	d.1934	No Mark
Son of Tawahongniwa. Started work at Carlisle. Demonstrated in San Diego in 1915.					
Lomawanu	Sun	Shungopavi	ca.1900	d. ca. 1913	No Mark
Son of Tawahongniwa.					
Silas Kewanwyma	Sun	Shungopavi	ca.1900	d.1932	No Mark
(Also: Silas Yma) Son of Tawahongniwa. Entered silver in 1930 Hopi Craftsman Show.					

HALLMARK	SILVERSMITH	CLAN	VILLAGE	BEGAN SILVER WORK	WORKED SILVER UNTIL
No Mark	Washington Talayumptewa	Sun	Shungopavi	ca.1900	1963 d.1963

(Also: Talaiumtewa) Son of Tawahongniwa. Continued silverworking until his death, but last entries in Hopi Craftsman Show were earrings of wood, inlaid with turquoise.

No Mark	Rutherford	Sun	Shungopavi	ca.1930s	1936 d.1962

(Also: Tongeva, Tonagive; Du-va-ma, Devayma, Durwyma) One of Tawahongniwa's five sons. Toured the United States demonstrating Hopi silversmithing, but made no more after he returned home.

No Mark	Dan Kochongva	Sun	Oraibi- Hotevilla	pre-1906	ca.1940s d.1972

(Also: Koitshongva, Kot-ka) Born in Oraibi but moved to Hotevilla at the Split. Half-brother of Sakhoioma. May be the Dan Kwiamawioma listed in Adair (1944:194) but no one seems to be familiar with the name.

No Mark	Sakhoioma	Sun	Oraibi- Hotevilla	pre-1906	ca.1950

Half-brother of Dan Kochongva. Moved to Hotevilla at the Split.

No Mark	Tenakhongva	Lizard	Oraibi- Hotevilla	ca.1900	date unknown

Moved to Hotevilla at the Split.

No Mark	Sakewyumptewa	Water- house	Oraibi- Hotevilla	ca.1907- 1912	d. after 1941

(nickname: Sió) Called Sió, meaning "The Zuñi," because he spent a lot of time at Zuni. I believe this is Adair's "Sakwiam."

Thundercloud & H (Hopi)	Ralph Tawangyaouma	Young Corn	Oraibi- Hotevilla	ca.1906	present

(Also: Tawagioma) Mark first used around 1930. Moved to Hotevilla at the Split. Did silversmithing in shops in Phoenix and Tucson until about 1964, when he moved back to Hotevilla.

No Mark	Pierce Kewanwytewa	Young Corn	Oraibi	ca.1906	d.1960

(Also: Kewawytewa, Kwomáyowma) Maternal first cousin of Ralph Tawangyaouma. Married a Zia woman around 1934 and moved to Zia, but continued to make silver.

No Mark	Bert Fredericks	Bear	Oraibi	ca.1900	1960s d.1960s

(Also: Sakwaitewa) Specialized in squash blossom necklaces and concha belts.

No Mark	Roscoe Nuvasi	unknown	Sichomovi	1915	1938

(Also: Narvasi) Nephew of Sikyatala. Father of Perry Nuvasi. Still working in 1938.

SILVERSMITH	CLAN	VILLAGE	BEGAN SILVER WORK	WORKED SILVER UNTIL	HALLMARK
Earl Numkina	Reed	Moencopi	ca.1920	1940s alive 1972	Man's Head Scarf

Taught himself to make silver. Demonstrated silverwork at the Chicago World's Fair. Eyes failed in the 1940s.

Frank Nutaima	Rabbit	Moencopi	pre-1920	1940s d.1966	No Mark

Did excellent cast as well as stamped work. Eyes failed in the 1940s.

Gene Nuvahoioma	Coyote	Oraibi-Hotevilla	1920s	alive 1972	No Mark

(Also: Jean; Nevahoioma, Nivowhioma; Pooyauma) Moved to Hotevilla at Split. Learned from Ralph, a first cousin of his wife, probably during 1920s. Was still working in 1930s. Son Allen Pooyama is a silversmith.

Titus Lamson	Saltbush	Hotevilla	ca.1925	1940s	No Mark

Still doing silverwork in 1940s.

Homer Vance	Sun	Shipaulovi	ca.1920	d.1961	Mark Not Definite

(Also: Humiventewa) Born 1882. Worked at Grand Canyon for a year, as well as other stores.

Harold Jenkins	Coyote	Oraibi-Moencopi	ca.1925	ca.1939 d.1949	No Mark

Learned from his brother-in-law, Frank Nutaima.

Grant Jenkins	Coyote	Oraibi-Moencopi	pre-1924	d. ca. 1935	Coyote Head & H

First cousin of Harold Jenkins. Worked for jewelry stores in Phoenix and Flagstaff.

Morris Robinson	Lizard	Oraibi-Bakabi	1924	present	Snake & H

(Also: Talawytewa, Tealanwytewa) Mark used ca. 1931. Lived with Grant Jenkins in Phoenix and began to work silver then. Worked for many years as silversmith in Phoenix. Retired in 1960s and returned to Bakabi. Did some cast work.

Randall Honwisioma	Parrot	Mishongnovi	pre-1934	1962	Parrot

(Also: Honwesima) Born 1906. Learned from Grant Jenkins at Graves Indian Store (later Skiles) in Phoenix. Worked for Vaughn's Indian Store in Williams, Arizona from 1937 to 1962. Now is almost blind.

Paul Saufkie	Snow	Shungopavi	1920s	present	Snow Cloud

(Also: Paul Andrew, Sifki) Son of Andrew Humiquaptewa. Learned from his father. Taught veterans' classes in silvermaking at Oraibi from 1948 to 1950. Made very little silver for fifteen years, but is starting again.

HALLMARK	SILVERSMITH	CLAN	VILLAGE	BEGAN SILVER WORK	WORKED SILVER UNTIL
No Mark	Ben Setema (Also: Setima)	Kachina	Oraibi	ca.1925	date unknown
No Mark	Arthur Masawytewa	Eagle	Mishongnovi	1930s	killed 1952

(Also: Arthur Hubbard) Was making silver in the 1930s. Entered silver in the 1930 Hopi Craftsman Show.

| No Mark | Robert Setalla | Millet | Walpi | 1933 | killed 1940 |

Born in Walpi, but married a woman of Moencopi. Made a large amount of jewelry as a wholesale supplier to retail stores. His wife, Laura Payestewa, helped a little at times.

| No Mark | Ferris Setalla | Millet | Walpi | 1933 | date unknown |

Both he and his brother Robert learned from Randall Honwisioma in Phoenix.

| No Mark | Harry A. Nasiwytewa | Coyote | Oraibi | 1930s | d.1950 |

Perhaps learned from Ralph Tawangyouma. Worked for stores in Phoenix. Was making silver in the 1930s.

| No Mark | Phillip Zi ayo ma, Jr. | unknown | Mishongnovi | ca.1930 | d.1960s |

(Also: Zeyouma) Made some silver when he had a store at the base of Mt. Elden in 1930, but later moved to Parker, Arizona.

| Snake & L. L. | Lewis Lomay | Masau | Oraibi | ca.1930 | present |

(Also: Lomayesva) Mark is from father's clan. Started silverwork at Santa Fe Indian School with Ambrose Roanhorse. Worked for Frank Patania's silvershop in Santa Fe for about 13 years. Now doing other work in Santa Fe. Was doing some cast work around 1949.

| No Mark | Walter Muchka | Badger | Oraibi | ca.1930 | killed 1938 |

Worked with Lewis Lomay for Frank Patania while in Santa Fe. Killed at age twenty-five.

| Masau | Willie Coin | Masau | Oraibi-Bakabi | 1930 | present |

(Also: Sitz wi isah) Used mark ca. 1948. Born in Oraibi, moved to Bakabi at marriage. Learned to make silver from his uncle, Earl Numkina, when they were acting in a San Gabriel Mission play in California.

| Thunderhead | Sidney Secakuku | Snow | Shungopavi | pre-1940 | date unknown |

Half-brother of Paul Saufkie and learned from him. Has not done silverwork for a long time.

SILVERSMITH	CLAN	VILLAGE	BEGAN SILVER WORK	WORKED SILVER UNTIL	HALLMARK
Allen Pooyama	Young Corn	Hotevilla	ca.1937	present	Ear of Corn

(Also: Pooyaouma, Nuvahoyouma) Learned from his father, Gene Nuvahoyouma. Did commercial silverwork in Tucson for many years, but moved to Holbrook in 1970.

Harry Sakyesva	Young Corn	Hotevilla	ca.1940s	d.1971	Tadpole

May have learned from Ralph Tawangyaouma and Allen Pooyama in Tucson. He was an excellent smith who continued to work though his health was very poor the last ten to fifteen years of his life.

Eddie Scott	Badger	Hotevilla	1937	killed 1951	No Mark

Learned from Allen Pooyama. Did commercial work in Flagstaff for Doc Williams' Saddlery Shop.

Marshall Jenkins	Bear	Oraibi-Bakabi	1939	present	Bear Claw

First used hallmark in 1967. Born Oraibi, moved to Bakabi at marriage. Learned from Chester Yellowhair at school in Albuquerque. Did little silverwork till 1960s when he moved from Navajo Ordnance Depot in Flagstaff back to Bakabi.

Preston Monongye	Saltbush	Hotevilla	1939	present	1950–1955 Peyote Rain Bird Initials 1965

Used first mark shown from 1950 to 1955. Now uses Peyote Rain Bird mark for some pieces, and since 1965, has used initials for his cast work. Works in gold, as well as silver.

Frieda Santiago	Masau	New Oraibi	late 1930s	ca.1964	No Mark

Daughter of Jessie Posiomana. Learned techniques from Willie Coin. Married a Zuñi man, Sylvester Santiago, and worked with him. They furnished Zuñi style jewelry for various Indian craft stores. Quit ca. 1964 because of impaired eyesight.

Victor Coochwytewa	Water-house	Shungopavi	1940	present	Rain Cloud

(Also: Victor Hugh) Originally worked with Paul Saufkie but also attended the veterans' classes. Has consistently made a quantity of jewelry for sale since then.

Valjean Joshevema	Sun	Shungopavi-Oraibi	1948 G.I. Bill	present	Crescent Moon

(Also: Lomaheftewa) Born Shungopavi, moved to Oraibi at marriage. Has started silverwork again in the last few years.

HALLMARK	SILVERSMITH	CLAN	VILLAGE	BEGAN SILVER WORK	WORKED SILVER UNTIL
Eagle	Tom Humiyestiwa	Eagle	Mishongnovi	1948 G.I. Bill	ca.1951
	Has done very little since veterans' classes.				
Tobacco Leaf	Everett Harris	Tobacco	Mishongnovi	1948 G.I. Bill	ca.1951 killed 1968
	Has done very little since veterans' classes.				
Star	Harold Koruh	Sun	Mishongnovi	1948 G.I. Bill	ca.1951
	Has done very little since veterans' classes.				
Pipe	Vernon Talas	Tobacco	Hano-Shungopavi	1948 G.I. Bill	present
	Born Hano, moved to Shungopavi at marriage. Had done blacksmithing before, so he made his own tools and some for others in the class. Is making a small amount now.				
Sun	Arthur Yowytewa	Sun	Oraibi-Bakabi	1948 G.I. Bill	1970
	Born Oraibi, moved to Bakabi at marriage. Quit in 1970 because of impaired eyesight.				
Antelope Rattle	Charles T. Lomakima	Bear-Strap	Shungopavi	1948 G.I. Bill	ca.1951
	Worked about two and a half years during the silver classes.				
Turtle	Eddie Nequatewa	Water-house	Shungopavi	1948 G.I. Bill	ca.1955
	Worked for about four years after veterans' classes.				
Bear	Travis Yaiva	Bear	Oraibi	1948 G.I. Bill	not at present

SILVERSMITH	CLAN	VILLAGE	BEGAN SILVER WORK	WORKED SILVER UNTIL	HALLMARK
Clarence Lomayestewa	Snow	Shungopavi	1948 G.I. Bill	1964	Killdeer Track (Patsrokuku)

Has given tools to his brothers, Mark and McBride.

Douglas Holmes	Badger	Moencopi-Shungopavi	1948 G.I. Bill	1961	Butterfly

Born Moencopi, moved to Shungopavi at marriage.

Henry Polingyouma	Sun's Forehead	Shungopavi-Oraibi	1948 G.I. Bill	ca.1951	Sun's Forehead

Born Shungopavi, moved to Oraibi at marriage. Worked only during veterans' classes.

Herbert Komayouse	Spider	Hotevilla	1948 G.I. Bill	date unknown	Spider

(Also: Quimayousie)

Lavern Siwingyumptewa	Water-house	Mishongnovi	1948 G.I. Bill	date unknown	Tadpole

Has given his tools to his brother Eldon. Has not done silverwork for some time.

Dean Siwingyumptewa	Water-house	Mishongnovi	1948 G.I. Bill	date unknown	Cloud

Brother of Lavern and Eldon. Has not done silverwork for some time. Has given his tools to his brother Eldon.

Orville Talayumptewa	Bear	Bakabi	1948 G.I. Bill	date unknown	Bear Paw

Neilson Honyaktewa	Snake	Mishongnovi-Shipaulovi	1948 G.I. Bill	ca.1951	Lizard

Born Mishongnovi, moved to Shipaulovi at marriage. Has not done silverwork since veterans' classes.

Calvin Hastings	Rabbit	Mishongnovi	1948 G.I. Bill	date unknown	Tobacco Flower

Has not done silverwork for some time.

HALLMARK	SILVERSMITH	CLAN	VILLAGE	BEGAN SILVER WORK	WORKED SILVER UNTIL
Crossed Arrows	Wallie Sekayumptewa	Reed	Hotevilla-Oraibi-Shungopavi	1948 G.I. Bill	1967
	Quit in 1967 because of impaired eyesight.				
Rattlesnake Head	Richard Kagenvema	Sun's Forehead	Shungopavi	1948 G.I. Bill	present
	(Pronounced: Kachin'-vema) Added the fangs to the head of his silvermark about 1969.				
Nahsompi (Hair Whorl)	Edgar Miller Hovalo	Kachina	Polacca-Mishongnovi	1948 G.I. Bill	d.1950s
	Born Polacca, moved to Mishongnovi at marriage.				
Sun	Samuel N. Laban	Sun's Forehead	Shipaulovi	1948 G.I. Bill	d. ca. 1955
Lightning	Dawson Numkina	Young Corn	Shipaulovi	1948 G.I. Bill	date unknown
Rattlesnake Rattle	Walter Polelonema	Sun's Forehead	Shungopavi	1948 G.I. Bill	killed 1971
	Worked until his death.				
War God	Cortez Lomahukva	Bear	Mishongnovi	1948 G.I. Bill	ca.1951
	(Also: Masayesva) Probably has not done silversmithing since veterans' classes.				
Bluebird	Starlie Lomayaktewa, Jr.	Bluebird	Mishongnovi	1948 G.I. Bill	date unknown
	Has not done silversmithing for some time.				

SILVERSMITH	CLAN	VILLAGE	BEGAN SILVER WORK	WORKED SILVER UNTIL	HALLMARK
Bert Puhuyestiwa	unknown	Mishongnovi	1948 G.I. Bill	date unknown	Crow Mother
Has not done silversmithing for some time.					
Kirkland Lomawaima	Squash	Shungopavi	1948 G.I. Bill	date unknown	Squash
Has not done silverwork for some time. Has given his tools away.					
Nielson Suetopke	Parrot	Hotevilla	1948 G.I. Bill	date unknown	Mark Unknown
Dewan Sumatzkuku	Coyote	Hotevilla	1948 G.I. Bill	ca.1951	Coyote
Didn't work after the veterans' classes.					
Edgar Coin	Rabbit	Oraibi	1948	date unknown	Tobacco Leaf
Did not attend veterans' classes.					
Ted Wadsworth	Bear	Shungopavi	1954	present	Rabbit Stick
(Also: Masungyouma) Brother-in-law of Victor Coochwytewa.					
Mark Lomayestewa	Snow	Shungopavi	1955	present	Snow Cloud
McBride Lomayestewa	Snow	Shungopavi	1955	present	Lightning
Brother of Mark and Clarence.					
Leroy Kewanyama	Water-house	Shungopavi	1955	present	Star Priest
Charles Loloma	Badger	Hotevilla	1955	present	Loloma
Born 1921. Worked with Bob Winston, Fred Skaggs, and Morris Robinson. Made pottery before he worked silver.					

HALLMARK	SILVERSMITH	CLAN	VILLAGE	BEGAN SILVER WORK	WORKED SILVER UNTIL
Bear	Lawrence Saufkie	Bear	Shungopavi	1947	present
	Born 1935. Son of Paul Saufkie. Learned from his father when a teen-ager. After marriage began to do more silverwork.				
Snow Cloud	Bernard Dawahoya	Snow	Shungopavi	1956	present
	Learned some from his uncles, Washington Talayumptewa and Sidney Secakuku. Then worked in the Guild Shop. Later worked for Hopicrafts when it opened in Phoenix and moved with them to the New Oraibi shop where he helped instruct their smiths. Now works for himself.				
Orion 1967 Two Feathers 1970	Vernon Mansfield	Sun	Shungopavi	1959	present
	He and Willard Nuvayaouma were first cousins. Willard gave him his tools and mark to use ca. 1967. Vernon had lost his mark, so started using the new one in 1970.				
Feather	Willard Nuvayaouma	Sun	Shungopavi	1959	killed 1969
	Hadn't done any silver work for some time previous to his death.				
Spider	Larson Onsae	Bear-Strap	Shungopavi	1957	1960s
	Was working in 1962, but not now.				
Star & Crescent Moon	Billie Ray Hawee	Sun	Shungopavi-Hotevilla	1959	present
	Born Shungopavi, moved to Hotevilla at marriage.				
SEKAQUAPTEWA	Wayne & Emory Sekaquaptewa	Eagle	New Oraibi	1960	present
	Learned from Harry Sakyesva. They own and manage the Hopi Enterprises, now Hopicrafts shop, which makes silver, as well as selling it wholesale and retail.				
Rabbit	Eldon James	Rabbit	Hotevilla-Shungopavi	1962	present
	Born Hotevilla, moved to Shungopavi at marriage. First worked at Hopicrafts when it opened in Phoenix, and moved with them to New Oraibi. Now works for himself.				

SILVERSMITH	CLAN	VILLAGE	BEGAN SILVER WORK	WORKED SILVER UNTIL	HALLMARK
Glenn Lucas	Sun	New Oraibi-Mishongnovi	ca.1966	present	

Born New Oraibi, moved to Mishongnovi at marriage. Learned at Hopicrafts and still works for them.

Gracilda Saufkie	Fog	Shungopavi	1964	present	Snow Cloud 1965

Learned from her husband, Lawrence. Broke her first mark in 1971 and used new one in 1972.

Snow Cloud 1972

Patrick Lomawaima	Snow	Shungopavi	1965	present	Snowflake 1965

Cloud 1967

Son of Kirkland Lomawaima. Lost the Snowflake mark and started using the Cloud in 1967.

Norman Honie	Spider	Hano-Shungopavi	1966	present	Spider

Born Hano, moved to Shungopavi at marriage.

Manuel Poseyesva	Snow	Shungopavi-Sichomovi	1965	1967	Snow Cloud

Born Shungopavi, moved to Sichomovi at marriage. Learned at Hopicrafts. Moved to Chicago in 1967.

Weaver Selina	Sun's Forehead	Shungopavi	1967	present	Sun's Forehead

Learned at Hopicrafts.

Phillip Honani	Bear	Shungopavi	1967	present	Friendship Mark

Learned at Hopicrafts.

HALLMARK	SILVERSMITH	CLAN	VILLAGE	BEGAN SILVER WORK	WORKED SILVER UNTIL
Cloud	Eldon Siwingyumptewa	Snow	Mishongnovi	1968	present
Ear of Corn	Franklin Namingha	Young Corn	Hotevilla-Shungopavi	1969	present
	Born Hotevilla, moved to Shungopavi at marriage.				
Antelope	Arlo Nuvayaouma	Bear	Shungopavi	1969	date unknown
	Not silverworking now. Living in Phoenix.				
Star	Dalton Taylor	Sun	Shungopavi	1970	present
Corn Plant	Kenneth Kuwanvayouma	Young Corn	Shungopavi	1970	present
Feather	Jackson Seklestewa	Eagle	Mishongnovi	1970	present
BG	Bradley Gashwazri	Rabbit	Oraibi-Mishongnovi	1963	present
	Born Oraibi, moved to Mishongnovi at marriage. Learned from Hopicrafts and still works for them.				
MS	Michael Sockyma	Young Corn	Hotevilla-New Oraibi	1965	present
	Born Hotevilla, moved to New Oraibi upon marriage. Learned at Hopicrafts and still works there.				

SILVERSMITH	CLAN	VILLAGE	BEGAN SILVER WORK	WORKED SILVER UNTIL	HALLMARK
Hubert Yowytewa	Reed	Bakabi	1965	present	HY Father's Sun Symbol

Learned from his father, Arthur Yowytewa, and at Hopicrafts. Uses his initials with his father's symbol.

SILVERSMITH	CLAN	VILLAGE	BEGAN SILVER WORK	WORKED SILVER UNTIL	HALLMARK
Tony Kyasyousie	Saltbush	Hotevilla	1969	present	TK

Learned at Hopicrafts and still works there.

| Gary Yoyokie | Coyote | New Oraibi | 1969 | present | No Mark to Date |

Learned at Hopicrafts. Graduated from high school in 1972 and has been working summers.

| Daniel Phillips | Saltbush | Oraibi | 1970 | present | |

Learned at Hopicrafts.

| Raymond Sequaptewa | Young Corn | Hotevilla | 1970 | present | Initials |

| Ross Joseyesva | Bear | Shungopavi | 1971 | present | No Mark to Date |

Worked a little with Lawrence Saufkie and then went to Hopi Guild.

| Andrew Saufkie | Bear | Shungopavi | 1971 | learning | No Mark to Date |

Son of Paul Saufkie.

| Joe Coochyumptewa | Rabbit | Mishongnovi | 1971 | learning | Pipe |

| unknown | | | ca. late 1940s | date unknown | |

HALLMARK	SILVERSMITH	CLAN	VILLAGE	BEGAN SILVER WORK	WORKED SILVER UNTIL
Ho JN	unknown			date unknown	date unknown
Sun	Hopi Silvercraft Guild		Second Mesa	1949	present

Each smith has his own Guild stamp. Consequently, none are exactly alike, as is shown in the few illustrated here. Mailing address is Second Mesa.

HALLMARK	SILVERSMITH	CLAN	VILLAGE	BEGAN SILVER WORK	WORKED SILVER UNTIL
Ht	Hopi Enterprises (See below.)			1961	1962
Ht	Hopicrafts		New Oraibi	1962	

Hopi silver shop owned by Wayne and Emory Sekaquaptewa. The business was first located in Phoenix and was called Hopi Enterprises. The workshop is now located at New Oraibi, and the salesroom is in the Hopi Cultural Center at Second Mesa.

Appendix I

WORKING SILVERSMITHS LISTED BY JOHN ADAIR IN 1938
Adair 1946, p. 194–195

At Moenkopi
  Harold Jenkins
  Earl Numkina
  Frank Nutaima
At Hotevilla
  Sakwiam
  Katchioma
  Jean Nivawhioma
  Titus Lamson
  Dan Kwiamawioma
At Bakavi
  Willie Coin
At Shongopavi
  Paul Saufki
  Washington Talaiumtewa

At Sichomovi
  Roscoe Narvasi

Outside the Reservation
  Ralph Tawagioma, of Hotevilla,
    works in Phoenix
  Bert Frederick, of Oraibi,
    works in Flagstaff
  Pierce Kewaytewa, of Oraibi,
    works in the pueblo at Zia
  Homer Vance, of Shipaulovi,
    works at Williams
  Randall Honowisioma, of Mishongnovi,
    works at Williams

WORKING SILVERSMITHS LISTED BY MARY-RUSSELL F. COLTON IN 1939
Plateau 12, p. 7

Bert Frederick
Randal Honwisioma
Pierce Kewanwytewa
Dan Koitshongva
Titus Lamson
Lewis Lomayesva
Harry A. Nosewytewa
Earl Numkina

Frank Nutaima
Jean Nuvahoyowma
Morris Robinson
Sakhoioma
Paul Sifki
Washington Talaiumptewa
Ralph Tawangyawma
Homer Vance

Note the difference in spelling the names of the smiths. This is common when attempts are made by researchers to spell Indian names in English.

Appendix 2

STANDARDS FOR NAVAJO, PUEBLO, AND HOPI SILVER

In announcing its standards for the Government mark for Navajo, Pueblo, and Hopi silver and turquoise products, the Indian Arts and Crafts Board makes the following statement:

Navajo, Hopi, and Pueblo silverwork, as an art and as a product with a "quality" market, has been overwhelmed by machine production. The Indian craftsman, struggling to compete in price with the machine-made and factory-made imitations, has in turn been forced to adopt a machine technique, while at the same time his wages or earnings have been depressed to the "sweat-shop" level. Quality has been sacrificed to that extreme where Indian jewelry has become hardly more than a curio or a souvenir.

There is being produced, though in relatively small quantity, Indian silver and turquoise work as fine as ever produced in the older days. And there are many Indian craftsmen who, if a quality market can be restored, will eagerly and capably produce work as good as the best of earlier times.

They cannot, however, produce it in price competition with factory output, machine output, and "bench-work" semi-machine output.

The Arts and Crafts Board has studied the situation thoroughly and has sought the counsel of Indians, of Indian traders, and of specialists in the marketing of craft products. The Board has reached the conclusion that the Government mark should be applied only to the finest quality of wholly genuine, truly hand-fashioned, and authentic Indian silver and turquoise products.

Use of the Government mark is not obligatory on any Indian, any factory, or any merchant. The Board has no power or purpose to forbid such production by time-saving methods and with machine stereotyped and stinted materials as now supplies the curio market. But for the production which is worthy of a fine Indian tradition, the Board will make available the Government certificate of genuineness and of quality; and the Board will seek to widen the existing "quality" market and to find new markets for such output as deserves the Government mark. In the measure of its success, the Board

94

will help to bring about a larger reward for a greater number of Indian craftsmen, and to save from destruction a noble, historic art, which under right conditions can have a long future.

JOHN COLLIER, *Chairman*
Indian Arts and Crafts Board
United States Department of Interior
Washington, D.C.

March 9, 1937

STANDARDS FOR NAVAJO, PUEBLO, AND HOPI SILVER AND TURQUOISE PRODUCTS

Subject to the detailed requirements that follow, the Government stamp shall be affixed only to work individually produced and to work entirely hand-made. No object produced under conditions resembling a bench-work system, and no object in whose manufacture any power-driven machinery has been used, shall be eligible for the use of the Government stamp.

In detail, Indian silver objects, to merit the Government stamp of genuineness, must meet the following specifications:

(1) Material — Silver slugs of 1 ounce weight or other silver objects may be used, provided their fineness is at least 900; and provided further, that no silver sheet shall be used. Unless cast, the slug or other object is to be hand hammered to thickness and shape desired. The only exceptions here are pins or brooches or similar objects; ear screws for ear rings; backs for tie clasps and chain, which may be of silver of different fineness and mechanically made.

(2) Dies — Dies used are to be entirely hand-made, with no tool more mechanical than hand tools and vise. Dies shall contain only a single element of the design.

(3) Application of dies — Dies are to be applied to the object with the aid of nothing except hand tools.

(4) Applique elements in design — All such parts of the ornament are to be hand-made. If wire is used, it is to be hand-made with no tool other than a hand-made draw plate. These requirements apply to the boxes for stone used in the design.

(5) Stone for ornamentation — In addition to turquoise, the use of other local stone is permitted. Turquoise, if used, must be genuine stone, uncolored by any artificial means.

(6) Cutting of stone — All stone used, including turquoise, is to be hand-cut and polished. This permits the use of hand- or foot-driven wheels.

(7) Finish — All silver is to be hand polished.

95

For the present the Arts and Crafts Board reserves to itself the sole right to determine what silver, complying with the official standards, shall be stamped with the Government mark.

JOHN COLLIER, *Chairman*

Approved March 9, 1937
  Harold L. Ickes,
    Secretary of the Interior.

"Gasoline and acetylene torches are permitted, since any industrious smith can acquire one, and their use does not in any way affect the quality or appearance of the finished product."

KENNETH M. CHAPMAN
*Special Consultant in
Indian Arts and Crafts*

Glossary

ANASAZI.   Prehistoric Pueblo Indians of northern Arizona and New Mexico.

ANNEAL.   To harden the silver by alternate heating and pounding.

BOLO TIE.   An ornament of silver, stone, or other material fastened onto a braided leather loop so that it slides up under the chin, leaving the two leather ends hanging in place of a tie (sometimes spelled *bola*).

BOW GUARD.   Wide leather strap worn on the left wrist, formerly to protect the arm from the bowstring. Usually decorated with a wide ornament of silver.

CONCHA.   Spanish term for shell. One of the ovals of a segmented silver belt or of a bridle. Also the belt itself. Now commonly called *concho*.

FLATTER.   One type of a large double-headed blacksmith's hammer that is flat on one side and pointed on the other.

FLUX.   A substance applied to surfaces to be soldered which frees them from oxides so that they may be joined and will adhere.

HOHOKAM.   Prehistoric Indians who lived in central and southern Arizona and made characteristic red-on-buff pottery.

INGOT.   A mass of metal cast in some convenient shape for storage or for use.

KACHINA.   A Hopi supernatural being who may be impersonated by masked men or represented by a carved doll.

KIKMONGWI.   Hopi village chief.

MANTA.   Spanish term for coarse cotton cloth. As now used by the Hopi, it refers to the handwoven black woolen square used as a dress.

MAPONI.   Hopi name for bow guard. The Navajo word is *ga-to* or *ke-toh*.

97

MASAU.   One of the Hopi chief kachinas. In one of his aspects is a deity of the underworld.

MATTE or MATTING.   The dull black background of Hopi overlay silver, as well as the process of texturing this background with a small chisel or die.

MIMBRES.   Prehistoric Indian group of southwestern New Mexico, noted for their black and white pottery, often with life forms.

NAHSOMPI.   Stylized hair knot used as a distinguishing feature on some warrior kachinas.

NUKWIVI.   Hopi hominy stew.

PIKI BREAD.   A paper-thin wafer bread made by the Hopi from corn flour, especially blue corn.

REPOUSSÉ: Decoration formed by a raised pattern beaten up from the reverse side.

SQUASH BLOSSOM NECKLACE.   A necklace composed of a large center pendant and eccentric beads placed at regular intervals among the round beads on either side of the center. The eccentric beads often have three or four petals on them and are called squash blossoms.

TEMPLATE.   A cut-out metal pattern used to trace the design onto the silver overlay piece.

Bibliography

Adair, John. *The Navajo and Pueblo Silversmiths.* Norman: University of Oklahoma Press, 1944.

Arizona Sun. Flagstaff: July 22, 1946.

Bahti, Tom. *Southwestern Indian Arts & Crafts.* Flagstaff: K. C. Publications, 1966.

Bartlett, Katharine. "Notes on the Indian Crafts of Northern Arizona." *Museum Notes* 10:22–24. Flagstaff: Museum of Northern Arizona, 1938.

Bedinger, Margery. *Navajo Indian Silver Work.* Old West Series of Pamphlets, no. 8. Denver: John Van Male, 1936.

Colton, Harold S. "Exhibitions of Indian Arts and Crafts." *Plateau* 12:60–65. Flagstaff: Museum of Northern Arizona, 1940.

Colton, Mary-Russell F. "Hopi Silversmithing — Its Background and Future." *Plateau* 12:1–7. Flagstaff: Museum of Northern Arizona, 1939.

Education Division, U.S. Indian Service. *Indian Education* Jan. 15, 1949, p. 8. Washington, D.C.

Hodge, F. W. "How Old is Southwestern Indian Silverwork?" *El Palacio* 25: 224–232. Santa Fe: Museum of New Mexico, 1928.

Kabotie, Fred. *Designs from the Ancient Mimbreños with a Hopi Interpretation.* San Francisco: Grabhorn Press, 1949.

_____. *Hopi Silver.* Mimeographed catalog. Oraibi, Arizona: Hopi Silvercraft Guild, 1950.

McGibbeny, J. H. "Hopi Jewelry." *Arizona Highways* July 1950, pp. 18–25.

Mera, Harry P. *Indian Silverwork of the Southwest.* Vol. 1. Globe, Arizona: Dale Stuart King, 1959.

Monongye, Preston. "The New Indian Jewelry Art of the Southwest." *Arizona Highways* June 1972, pp. 7–10.

Nequatewa, Edmund. *Truth of a Hopi.* Flagstaff: Museum of Northern Arizona, Bulletin 8 (1936; reprint ed. 1967).

Plateau. "Dr. Harold Sellers Colton 1881–1970." 43:146–147. Flagstaff: Museum of Northern Arizona,1971.

Plateau. "Mary-Russell Ferrell Colton 1889–1971." 44:38–40. Flagstaff: Museum of Northern Arizona, 1971.

Ritzenthaler, Robert E. "Hopi Indian Silverwork." *Lore* 16:92–98. Milwaukee: Milwaukee Public Museum, 1966.

Indian Arts and Crafts Board, Dept. of Interior. *Smoke Signals.* Feb. 1963, p. 10. Washington, D.C.

Stephens, Alexander M. *Hopi Journal.* Edited by Elsie Clews Parsons, 2 vols. New York: Columbia University Press, 1936.

Stevenson, James. *Illustrated Catalogue of the Collections Obtained from the Indians of New Mexico and Arizona in 1879.* Second Annual Report 1880–1881, Smithsonian Institution. Washington, D.C.: Publications of the Bureau of Ethnology, 1883.

Stevenson, James. *Illustrated Catalogue of the Collections Obtained from the Pueblos of Zuñi, New Mexico, and Wolpi, Arizona in 1881.* Third Annual Report 1881–1882, Smithsonian Institution. Washington, D.C.: Publications of the Bureau of Ethnology, 1884.

Tanner, Clara Lee. "Contemporary Southwest Indian Silver." *Kiva* 25, no. 3, pp. 1–22. Tucson: Arizona State Museum, 1960.

_____. "Crafts of Arizona Indians." *Arizona Highways* July 1960, pp. 8–35.

_____. *Southwest Indian Craft Arts.* Tucson: University of Arizona Press, 1968.

Thompson, Laura and Joseph, Alice. *The Hopi Way.* 2nd ed. Chicago: University of Chicago Press, 1947.

Titiev, Mischa. *Old Oraibi, A Study of the Hopi Indians of Third Mesa.* Papers of the Peabody Museum of American Archaeology and Ethnology, vol. 22, no. 1. Cambridge: Peabody Museum, 1944.

Underhill, Ruth. *Here Come the Navajo.* Haskell, Kansas: United States Indian Service, 1953.

Whiting, Alfred F. *Hopi Arts and Crafts Survey for the Indian Arts and Crafts Board.* 4 vols. Flagstaff: Museum of Northern Arizona Archives, 1942.

Woodward, Arthur. *Navajo Silver: A Brief History of Navajo Silversmithing.* 1938. New ed. Flagstaff: Northland Press, 1971.

Wright, Barton A. "The Role of Tradition in Indian Crafts." *Tenth Scottsdale National Indian Arts Exhibition Catalog,* 1971, pp. 14–15.

Index

Victor Coochwytewa 43, 56, 66, 67, 70, 83, 86

Wadsworth, Ted 70, 87
Wallie Sekayumptewa 66, 86
Walter Muchka 82
Walter Polelonema 86
Washington Talayumptewa 16, 44, 67, 80, 87
Wayne Sekaquaptewa 59, 60, 67, 88
Weaver Selina 57,89

Willard Nuvayaouma 88
Willie Coin 26, 28, 29, 71, 82, 83

Yaiva, Travis 48, 84
Yellow Light. *See* Sikyatala
Yowytewa, Arthur 39, 84, 90
Yowytewa, Hubert 91
Yoyokie, Gary 91

Zi ayo ma, Phillip 82